The New Radical

How the protests of the sixties became a message for today

The story of an activist for peace, community, racial integration, the poor . . .

'This book is the story of my personal pilgrimage from America's evangelical heartland to a crisis of faith, through the civil rights and anti-war movements of the 1960s to a recovery of personal faith in Jesus Christ and his radical message of the kingdom of God.'
Jim Wallis

JIM WALLIS

THE NEW RADICAL

A LION PAPERBACK

Copyright © 1983 Abingdon Press,
Nashville, Tennessee, USA

Published by
Lion Publishing plc
Icknield Way, Tring, Herts, England
ISBN 0 85648 594 2
Albatross Books Pty Ltd
PO Box 320, Sutherland, NSW 2232, Australia
ISBN 0 86760 471 9

First UK edition 1983
Reprinted 1986

British Library Cataloguing in Publication Data
Wallis, Jim
  The new radical.
  1. Christian Life
  I. Title
  248.4   BV4501.2
  ISBN 0 85648 594 2

Printed and bound in Great Britain by
Cox & Wyman Ltd, Reading

*For my parents
and to the memory of A. P. Gibbs
and the other evangelists of my tradition
who kept the gospel alive.*

Acknowledgements

Thanks for this book go especially to Joyce
Hollyday, who helped from beginning to end
with the writing, rewriting, and editing. With
gentle persistence, she pulled out of me many
of the old stories and anecdotes that appear
in the book. Her companionship in the work,
marked by warm encouragement, faithfulness
to the task, and a sense of humour, kept me
going when a much too busy schedule could
have easily sidetracked the project.

Thanks also go to Lindsay McLaughlin,
who brought her characteristic quality and
good spirit to the copy editing. Susan Masters
graciously typed the manuscript with help
from other magazine staff members.

Because the book is, in part, a story of
Sojourners, everyone who has ever been
involved in the fellowship helped shape the
story that is here told.

Contents

Introduction

It was a hot August night in Chicago twelve years ago. I was standing in the main pressroom of the city's cheapest printer, a countercultural character who had told our little group he liked what we were trying to do and had promised to give us "a good deal."

Stacked on the floor all around me were the publications of other customers. The *Black Panther*, which was thriving at the time, dominated the space. It was surrounded by all the little tabloids in Polish and Spanish and half a dozen other languages, which carried the news and gossip of Chicago's incredibly diverse ethnic neighborhoods.

I saw that our layout boards had been made into plates. Just a few weeks before, I hadn't known what layout boards were, and a dozen other terms of journalistic jargon still remained foreign to me. The plates were put on the press, the ink wells were filled, and a roll of fresh-smelling newsprint was put in. Then the presses began to roll, and I could see all our hopes, sweat, and prayers coming to fruition.

Seven of us had scraped together a hundred dollars each to make this dream come true. Bob Sabath had typeset this first issue of the *Post-American*, the forerunner of *Sojourners*, on an archaic typesetter rented from an underground newspaper. We had only twenty-five dollars from our small budget to put toward the task—the price of a night's rental.

We were up all night using the typesetter during the only hours the underground paper wasn't. Bob banged out the copy while the rest of us proofread. Throughout the night we endured the blasts of a band from a singles' bar below and the regular intrusion of the elevated train that passed by just fifteen feet away.

Now I was witnessing the large printing press in operation, and I was fascinated. The night crew had let me come in to watch, no doubt smiling to themselves about this fellow who wanted to be there to make sure everything came out all right. They told me it would be done "sometime after ten." As I would learn many times after that, this printer's schedule was often a little loose.

When the first copy of the *Post-American* rolled off that big web press at 2:30 A.M., I was at the end of the line waiting for it. The ink was still wet when I picked it up and exclaimed, "It's beautiful!" I waited until the first bundle was finished, put it under my arm, and headed home, promising our return the next day to pick up the rest.

As I drove home that night, my mind was filled with thoughts and hopes. Every time I stopped for a traffic light I would hold up a copy of the sixteen-page tabloid again and look at it.

Halfway home I pulled into a gas station. While my tank was being filled, I walked up to three teen-agers who were sitting on the curb by the station's office and handed each of them a copy of the brand new publication, announcing proudly, "You are the first people ever to receive a copy of the *Post-American!*" Their bleary, drug-dazed eyes slowly scanned what had just been handed to them, and as they thumbed through its pages I nervously awaited our first public response.

One kid spied the price printed in the corner, looked at me, and said, "Only a quarter for this thing!" I was elated. Another reached into his pocket, no doubt to pull out a quarter. "No, no, no," I insisted, "for you this is free." (And ever since, our publisher, Joe Roos, tells me I give away too many complimentary copies.)

By the time I reached home it must have been four in the morning. Everyone was asleep in the house that had become our little community's home that first summer together in

1971. I crept up the stairs, making my way through the darkness to my bed, being careful not to awaken the two other guys with whom I shared the room. I put the bundle down, put a copy on the bed, and just stared at it.

After a few moments, I dropped to my knees and slowly began to pray. Strong feelings of gratitude, expectation, and bold, confident faith rushed over me. I remember a very powerful sense that something much larger than the efforts of our tiny group was at work here, and that the publication of this little tabloid held possibilities that I could not yet imagine. To this day that sense has never died.

We knew there had to be other people who were feeling the same things we were about the meaning of biblical faith in our time. In fact, that's why we decided to put out a publication: to articulate the new understanding of the gospel that was emerging among us and to reach out to others who found themselves engaged in the same struggles.

Though we were hopeful about the response, we were thoroughly unprepared for the amount of mail we received. Subscriptions began to pour in, and soon the shoebox we had set aside for the purpose of our record-keeping couldn't contain all the names of the new subscribers and friends we were finding around the country. We received phone calls, visits, and invitations. The *Post-American* had sparked something.

I have sometimes likened the publication of the *Post-American* to the raising of a flag up a flagpole. Many people on the ground, at the grass roots, were longing for an alternative to the narrow versions of Christian faith they were experiencing in their churches, but they didn't know one another. Many of the earliest letters to us expressed people's long-held feelings of being alone in their beliefs, wondering if any other Christians like them existed. People from many places saw the flag and met one another around the flagpole. From its first days, the magazine created an ecumenical spirit among people, bringing together those who had never before been in relationship.

The cover of the first issue was dramatic: a picture of Jesus wrapped in an American flag, with the crown of thorns on his head. It carried the caption, ". . . and they crucified Him." The message was clear. Jesus was being crucified again by our American Christianity. His gospel had become almost completely lost in a church that had become captive to its culture and trapped by a narrow vision of economic self-interest and American nationalism. Any real witness to the kingdom of God or practical demonstration of obedient discipleship in our day had all but disappeared from the churches.

The brutality of the war in Vietnam, the persistence of white racism, and the grinding oppression of the poor all screamed to heaven over the church's silence. A pervasive American civil religion was in fact sanctioning these manifold national sins, and the prophetic character of biblical faith was seldom invoked.

At least that was the experience of the church for those of us who put out the first issue of the *Post-American*. Most of us had been raised in the evangelical heartland of the country. The gospel message that had nurtured us as children was now turning us against the injustice and violence of our nation's leading institutions and causing us to repudiate the church's conformity to a system that we believed to be biblically wrong.

The message of the early issues of the *Post-American* was strident and soon became very controversial. In its pages, young evangelical Christians were calling the war in Vietnam a national sin and disgrace. There were other evangelical Christians in the land, and there were others who thought the war in Vietnam was wrong. But in 1971 there were very few evangelical Christians who were, on the basis of their faith, publicly opposing the war.

Looking back, there is nothing very new in what we were saying. It certainly wasn't as new as we thought it was at the time. *Sojourners* has always been in the historical stream of radical Christian orthodoxy. The oldest and best traditions of the church demand that the gospel be proclaimed and lived in the midst of the suffering world, that those who would follow

Jesus Christ be particularly sensitive to the poor and the oppressed. Those traditions remind us that the way of Jesus is the way of peace, and that a commitment to social justice is simply a consequence of biblical faith. The recovery of the gospel, the revival of the teaching of Jesus, and the renewal of the prophetic biblical tradition are commitments that have emerged again and again in the history of the church.

As the magazine grew, we discovered communities, movements, and explosions of faith from the past that served as precedents and guiding examples for our own experience. In the evangelical tradition, great social evils such as slavery, industrial exploitation, and discrimination against women were attacked on the basis of faith by revival movements in eighteenth-century England and nineteenth-century America. Through these forebears, we learned that it was not radical Christian faith that was heretical, but the church's conformity to American civil religion.

Today, the most perceptive social commentators among us consistently point to the fact that our problems are more than just political. A world brutally divided between rich and poor, a physical environment being subjected to a slow technological death, the possibility of nuclear destruction never more than a half hour away, and the world's burgeoning population perilously divided by race, class, and sex all point to the need for change in our most fundamental values more than for mere reforms in public policy. Even secular commentators recognize the necessity for some kind of spiritual transformation—a change in our basic sensibilities, the way that we think and feel about ourselves and the world.

The times cry out for a dramatic change in our relationship to our neighbor, to the earth, and, at root, to God. In more evangelical language, the crisis in which we now find ourselves—politically, economically, and spiritually—calls for revival.

We've seen the kind of revival before that rekindles faith and transforms the way people think, live, and act. Genuine revivals in times past decisively and profoundly changed the historical circumstances in which they occurred.

That conservative evangelical faith leads to conservative politics is a popular misconception. The historical and theological evidence shows otherwise. The greatest social movements in our own history—the struggles for American independence, abolition of slavery, civil rights, and women's suffrage—were in large part products of evangelical revivalism.

This book is the story of my personal pilgrimage from America's evangelical heartland to a crisis of faith, through the civil rights and antiwar movements of the 1960s, and finally to a recovery of personal faith in Jesus Christ and his radical message of the kingdom of God. It is the odyssey of a midwestern American boy born from the evangelical womb, who lost his faith, took on a secular pilgrimage, and then returned home to the tradition that bore him.

After years of spiritual formation and political education in the two most prominent social movements of our time, I returned home not to the evangelical subculture in which I was raised but to the powerful evangelical tradition from which I had sprung. I discovered that the power of biblical faith known so well by revivalists and reformers down through the years has the capacity to radically critique and challenge the root assumptions of American wealth and power. I sensed the possibility of the redirection of the evangelical tradition back to its most authentic stream, away from the culture-conforming detours it has taken in our country.

I realized that my evangelical faith, so long captive to American privilege and power, need not be abandoned after all, but rather recovered, rekindled, and restored to its truest meaning. I came to believe that the most radical evangelical impulses, like hot coals on a dying fire, might be fanned back into flames.

1
A Son of
the American Dream

World War II was good for patriotism. The American men who returned from its theaters of battle were honored as heroes and celebrated as victors. Uncle Sam welcomed them home with the promise that he would take care of his loyal nephews who had so valiantly fought in the great war.

Some went to college on the GI Bill. Many received help from the Federal Housing Administration to buy their first home.

Huge tracts of FHA-financed houses sprang up almost overnight after the war. Row upon row of small houses on small lots, identical outside except for the color of the brick, appeared in many corners of America. My family's was a gray, three-bedroom ranch house in Redford Township, Michigan.

Our working- and middle-class neighborhood on the edge of Detroit was filled with families just like ours. They were young, just getting started. Children seemed to be everywhere, and I had no lack of friends.

We grew up playing ball in the streets and running around what we called "the woods" at the end of the block. It was actually a big ravine that had been transformed into a dump, but to us it held all the adventure of Sherwood Forest and more.

I often went bow-and-arrow hunting there for crows, though I don't remember hitting one. My boyhood hero was Robin Hood. I read the story over and over, went to all the movies about him, and faithfully watched the television series.

Taking from the rich and giving to the poor seemed like a good idea to me.

At the head of each home in our neighborhood was a father who had risked his life to fight for the American Dream. In many ways, my father embodied that dream. The chapters of his life read like an American success story.

He was a track star, a top student, and president of his high school class. He married whom he thought was "the prettiest girl in the class." Their wedding, his graduation from the University of Michigan, and his commissioning as an officer in the U.S. Navy all occurred on the same day.

It was no surprise that he would go off with the navy to fight in the war. He believed in his God, his country, and his way of life. He was fair, faithful, and proud, and he always wanted to do what was right and what was best. He was at heart an idealist.

When he returned from the war, he went to work as a mechanical engineer for Detroit Edison. An ambitious and hard worker, he moved quickly up the company ladder. With each climb, he became less an engineer and more a businessman, and he is now an executive with the company.

My mother is a businesswoman in her own right, though for years she worked full time as a housewife and mother. When she has worked outside the home, it has usually been as an executive secretary. She has always moved quickly into places of responsibility, and I have often thought that, had she had the kind of education and training that my father did, she would have gone far in the business world.

My parents and their generation were formed by two pivotal events: the Great Depression and World War II. During the Depression, my mother's family lost everything they had. From the stories she told us, it was a very painful experience in all their lives. My father's family somehow managed to hang on but never by very much. All their friends and relatives felt the Depression very acutely.

The experience of losing everything and becoming poor created in my parents' generation a tremendous desire for economic security and a very deep fear of economic insecurity. In the postwar years, that led to a relentless pursuit of material affluence, success, and comfort which deeply shaped the lives of my parents and their friends, and the life of our church. They all wanted the good life, and they feared they might not attain it.

America after World War II offered a dream brighter than ever before. We ruled the world. The economy was booming. Our standard of living became the envy of the rest of the nations. It seemed to many that God had surely blessed us. Our national righteousness was evident in our wartime victory and peacetime prosperity. There was plenty for all who were upright in character and willing to work hard enough to succeed.

But, like our parallel pursuit of military security, there was never enough. The more we stockpiled possessions and weapons, the more insecure we became. Accumulation and armaments did not bring us security. It was all an illusion.

Had we read the Bible more carefully, we would not have been surprised. Biblically, security is found in the presence of justice and peace. The all-embracing pursuit of material success and comfort distorted our priorities, our faith, our church and family life. We were captivated, seduced, and captured by the materialism of post-World War II America.

If the reaction to the Depression was a frenzied pursuit of affluence in my parents' generation, the response to the success of World War II was unbridled nationalism. The years of my growing up were the peak of American power in the world. We had our way—always. We were the strongest, richest, and, we thought, most righteous country in the history of the nations. For all the fear of the Soviets, there was no one in the world who could pose a serious challenge to American dominance.

The anti-communism which followed World War II was pervasive. It became almost a religious cause and served as a convenient cover for American commercial, political, and military adventures all over the world. No matter what our country did, no matter how we intervened in the affairs of other countries, no matter how much suffering our policies brought, the great cause of anti-communism was invoked, and every act of political subversion, economic imperialism, or military aggression became justified and even took on the noble character of a righteous crusade.

The church eventually became corrupted by the twin ideologies of American nationalism and strident anti-communism. We became, in reality, American patriots first and Christians second. The church and its religion became tied to the nation's destiny.

Predictably, we became conformed to an American civil religion that was indeed religious, but hardly biblical. We began to defend America more than the gospel, and made the gospel subservient to the goals of the nation. There was no question in anyone's mind that to be faithful to both God and country was an easy thing to do in America, because God's purposes and our country's destiny were so closely linked.

I grew up being taught and believing that we were the greatest nation in history. We were a generous people, a blessed people, in fact, God's chosen people. America was constantly referred to as the "New Israel," a nation that had a special place in the history of the nations and in God's plan for the world. God had a special stake in America and had given us the particular responsibility of defending Christian values against the godless ideology of atheistic communism.

I was my parents' first child, part of the generation that was defined by the war. We were children conceived in victory who made up the ranks of the "postwar baby boom."

I was an all-American boy—born and raised an evangelical, middle-class, white kid in the Midwest. Four younger siblings—Barb, Bill, Terry, and Marcie—eventually joined the family, as well as a dog and assorted other pets, so my experience of community came early.

My parents are both kind and generous, and hospitality was an important part of our lives. Ours was the house in the neighborhood where all our friends stayed over. Even when the house was overrun and overflowing with kids, my mother seemed not to mind—and even to enjoy—being a mother to all. She was a loving and trusted figure in the lives of many of our friends.

Our doors were open to a variety of people. In more recent years, since all of us kids have grown up and left, the house has often been filled with people who need a place to stay—the college student, the friend of the family, the troubled teen-ager, the family left homeless by a fire.

I remember what seemed like a constant stream of people coming to the house to talk with my parents about their personal, spiritual, or marital problems. Most of them were from our church.

Plymouth Brethren churches, or assemblies as they are called, have no clergy, and the pastoral tasks and leadership are shared by a group of elders elected from the laymen of the local church. For most of my growing-up years, my father functioned as the chief elder of the church. So while he was an engineer and businessman, he also had a ministry of preaching and teaching, marrying and burying, and I had the experience of being raised as a preacher's kid.

My parents have for years done counseling and together led "marriage enrichment" courses for couples from the church. Both are pastors in reality, but only my father can serve and be officially recognized as one, because the role of women in the Plymouth Brethren Church is thoroughly subordinate. Women must keep their heads covered and are not allowed to speak in the services or to provide any kind of official leadership whatsoever, except with children and other women. Yet the fact is that in many ways the women held the church together.

My mother was one of those women. When my father performed a wedding, he'd be in charge of the ceremony and she'd be responsible for the reception. It seemed as if she organized most of the events that occurred in the life of the church: baby showers, Sunday school picnics, potluck dinners. But more importantly, she offered compassionate and spiritually grounded leadership to many who came to her for guidance.

My parents' concern for other people set a family style and tone. We were taught always to favor the underdog and were reminded to befriend the child with whom no one else wanted to play. I remember quite clearly how my parents rebuked the "colored jokes" we kids brought home from our friends and their parents, teaching us early that it was wrong to make fun of people for the color of their skin.

But their response to institutional racism was very different. When their country or its system was accused of being racist, they became defensive. They had a personal view of everything, which left them virtually unaware of the social, economic, and political injustices of America.

Like most parents, mine made the loving mistake of trying to protect their children from the world's unpleasant realities. Their lives revolved around the family, the church, and the workplace so that they were protected from facing the painful facts about America and were isolated from the victims of the system they trusted. Even their sincerely held Christian commitments became conditioned by the church's civil religion, which blessed the political and economic status quo.

My parents' view of the world confirmed their own values. Yet even during my most severe disagreements with them, when I was choosing other values, I knew that they loved me and would sacrifice greatly on my behalf. We made it through many stormy years together.

I remember coming home for a short weekend visit during my college years. Michigan State University had just been the scene of a series of antiwar demonstrations, and I had been in the thick of them. My father had been reading newspaper accounts of "the trouble" on campus, and he was particularly upset by his eldest son's role in the "disturbances."

My father trusted our nation's leaders. He believed he had fought for freedom in World War II, and he remembered friends who hadn't made it home from the war. This country had been good to him and his family. He couldn't understand why his son would turn against his views and believe, just as strongly, that the same country was guilty of terrible crimes against the Vietnamese, the poor, the blacks.

He took it personally. How had he failed in my upbringing? Who was responsible for my radical thinking? His resentment of my protest had been growing, and he was angry.

I sensed it was not a time to argue. I said I would give him the names of two persons most responsible for my present feelings and commitments. My father sat down, expecting to hear the names of some radical figures from the headlines, of some left-leaning professors on my campus. He was astounded when I told him that the two people who bore major responsibility for my disconcerting behavior were he and my mother.

"You taught me to care about people and their hurts. You bred in me a special concern for those who suffer most. Where do you think I learned the value of honesty and integrity? Of facing up to even the most difficult problems and questions? Most of all, of standing up for what I believe to be right, no matter who disagrees?"

In many ways, I said, I was trying to be consistent with his and my mother's own values. I was trying to apply them to the world as I saw it, a different world from the one they saw. My father sat speechless.

It had been two decades since he had named his first son after himself. It was a typical practice of the times to name the eldest son after the father, with great hopes that he would be just like his dad and carry on the family tradition.

For several years, I followed his lead. I looked up to my father and wanted to be just like him. He had the respect of many people, so it was natural that I would want to follow in his footsteps.

Until the age of thirteen, I was a perfect son. I was what I was supposed to be, which means I was a success—a good student and athlete, a leader in student government and in church activities. I was a Boy Scout senior patrol leader and the spelling bee champion of the sixth grade. I grew up with a baseball mitt on my left hand and was the captain of my Little League team.

The feeling of wanting to be the best dominated every area of my life. The success ethic and pressure to do well were strong in my home, and the pursuit of affirmation and excellence were of the greatest importance. My parents, teachers, coaches, Scout leaders, and church elders were never short on praise and pride about my accomplishments. The world seemed to me to be a very positive and friendly place.

Despite all my successes, I lived with a continual fear of failure. I developed a stutter, which became a large problem for both me and my family. Years of speech therapy never got rid of the stutter. It was a constant fear and preoccupation, making me especially self-conscious when I had to speak in front of others.

The stutter did not diminish until years later, though to this day it still remains a sort of thorn in the flesh. The problem is ironic, because my vocation has so much to do with the public articulation of the gospel.

I still think about the stutter every time I speak in public and I realize that the old fear hasn't left me. It is a continual reminder of my frailty and vulnerability. Most importantly, it is a reminder of my dependence on God.

Yet my fears were little known to the people around whom I grew up, who would have given me their vote for most likely to succeed. This was especially true of the leaders of the church.

As the firstborn son of the pastor, I thought it only natural that I should be involved in everything in the church. I was the only boy who went to the men's prayer meetings, not because I was particularly spiritual, but because I enjoyed the affirmation. From time to time, one of the elders would pat me on the head and say, "He's going to be a leader of this church some day."

Evangelicals are famous for coming up with contests to help kids learn the Bible. In Sunday school we often had "sword drills." We would sit at attention with our Bibles (our "swords") closed in hand, waiting for the Sunday school teacher to call out a scripture—chapter and verse. The first to find it in the Bible, stand up, and read it, would win and be rewarded. I was one of the fastest.

We once had a contest in Daily Vacation Bible School, a sort of summer Sunday school that ran every day for two weeks, to see who could come up with the most names for God. I paged through all my father's commentaries and dictionaries—most of his theological library—and found literally hundreds of names for God, including Greek and Hebrew ones. I think I did a bit of padding using "The God of Abraham," "The God of Isaac," "The God of Jacob," the God of as many Old Testament names as I could think of.

I won first prize: a parakeet. I remember that it had a rather nasty temperament. A few weeks after it joined our family, it dive-bombed my sister and knocked a glass of lemonade out of her hand on to the carpet. The parakeet was gone the next day; we gave it to the kid who came in second.

The revival tradition was strong in our church. During revival time you turned your life over to Christ, or renewed your commitment. This was especially important if you were guilty of "backsliding." Anything from dancing to not praying enough could qualify as a good backslide.

No one had more spiritual authority than the preacher who came from outside the church to lead the revival. Having him come and stay in your home was part of a long and legendary evangelical tradition. It was important to make a good impression.

Our family's hospitality often extended to these itinerant revivalists who came to town. I particularly remember A. P. Gibbs, my favorite of the great roving evangelists to take a meal at our table and rest in one of our beds. Before his arrival, my mother carefully schooled us in our table manners and warned us to be on our best behavior. We were all very nervous when the great preacher came to sit down at the table, trying our hardest to be the most well-mannered evangelical angels this side of heaven.

A. P. Gibbs was a stout man with a great mustache. He lumbered up to the table like he had been there before. We kids carefully watched every move he made.

He spied a bowl of grapes in the center of the table. Giving us a wink, he took a handful and began to pop them one by one into the air. Our eyes stayed fixed on the grapes, following their arc and watching them drop into his great preacher's mouth. Hardly believing what we saw, we sat wide-eyed, thrilled by his great skill. Then he asked if we wanted to try it too.

Before long we were all popping grapes into the air, laughing and watching them roll off the sides of our mouths and on to the floor, in most cases missing our mouths completely. My poor mother could only laugh as she witnessed this spectacle of havoc around her dinner table, orchestrated by the great preacher and followed by all her children, until finally nothing but stems were left in the bowl and grapes surrounded the table.

Everything about an outside preacher, especially his idiosyncrasies, was fascinating. A. P. Gibbs had more than the usual share. I remember that he would eat his soft-boiled eggs only out of an egg cup. We had never seen that before, and were as taken by it as by his grape-throwing skill. We were so enthralled that he went out and bought all of us kids our own egg cups so we could try it too.

A. P. Gibbs was a songwriter as well as a preacher. I recall after dinner reaching for his suitcase to carry it to the bedroom we had set aside for him. He was in the process of writing a new songbook, and the suitcase was filled with books and papers too heavy for me to lift. The papers soon found their way to every part of his bedroom, strewn from one end to the other—just as his laundry soon hung all over our bathroom from shower to sink.

Gibbs was typical of the best of the evangelical tradition. He was a genuine servant, a bachelor who gave his whole life to his ministry. He crisscrossed the United States spending a week here, two weeks there, a month somewhere else, at small churches ministering God's Word.

He was not given to comfort or idle leisure, vain speculations, or the kind of power and pomp of many evangelical preachers today. He lived very simply and would have been horrified at the kind of materialism that has now overtaken the church.

Though he was self-taught, he knew his Bible very well. And it was evident that he loved it. He could make you love the Bible too and want to be a better Christian. When he preached, the Word of God came alive.

Though he could preach a fiery sermon, he had a very gentle and tender heart. He seemed to have a special love for children, and would always make room in his busy schedule of study, sermon preparation, and book work for conversations with a little boy who would peer around the half-open door to his room to see if he were there.

Gibbs had a deep love for his Lord and love for the people of God. Though he was quite a character, full of personality, he had a noticeable humility about him. One saw none of the sort of empire building one finds today among the television preachers.

He moved from home to home, freely accepting hospitality, never having a home of his own. Like the Master he served, he had nowhere to lay his head. As far as I know, he had no property, wealth, or economic security, but he had a very important place in the hearts of the many people to whom he ministered.

A. P. Gibbs died an old man in a car accident while hurrying to his next city to preach. It is believed that he probably fell asleep at the wheel and the car went off the road. At the end, he had nothing to show for his life except the gratitude of One who must have said to him, "Well done, thou good and faithful servant," and the warm thankfulness of the people he served.

Churches like the one I grew up in needed people like A. P.

Gibbs to fire the soul and rekindle the lukewarm heart, to teach the Word until it burned within again. Periodic revivals were central to our understanding of religion; we knew we needed them.

Summer Bible camp filled a similar need. Bair Lake Bible Camp in Jones, Michigan, holds memories for me as one of the warmest places I knew growing up. The camp had the feel of a family, and the kids I spent those summer weeks with year after year became some of my closest friends.

My first love of course was the sports. But everyone knew that the main event at camp was the campfires. There were two or three a week, and they were times for "giving your testimony." Nothing was more important to an evangelical kid than having a testimony and being able to give it well.

As we became teen-agers, the testimonies got better and better. Kids would tell long tales of woe, how they had tried to live for the Lord this year at school, but just hadn't been able to do it. They had fallen in with the wrong crowd, began to backslide, and got into trouble. But with tears in their eyes, they would pledge that, thanks to their time this summer at Bair Lake, the next school year was going to be different. The next year at camp the testimony would be repeated.

Children's meetings were also part of our growing up. They were yearly occurrences, full of fiery preaching and altar calls. An altar call, for those of you who have never walked down that evangelical aisle, comes at the end of a sermon when the preacher gives the invitation to come forward and be saved or recommit your life to Christ—usually while the congregation is singing endless verses of "Just as I Am, Without One Plea" (just to make sure there is time for everyone to come forward).

Of course the purpose of the children's meetings was to get the kids saved. We were all the sons and daughters of Christian parents, but there were always many who had not yet made a "profession of faith." And it often took the stimulus of an outside preacher to bring about a conviction and decision for Christ.

I was saved when I was a six-year-old. I remember being scared to death by a Sunday night evangelist who told us kids that the Lord would come and take our parents to heaven, away from us, and that we would be left alone. I realized that I would have to support a five-year-old sister and a one-year-old brother. It was the awful prospect of being left alone with that task, separated from Mom and Dad, that caused me to repent of the sin and degradation of my first six years and to believe in Jesus. That was the beginning of my conversion. The cost of discipleship wasn't raised that night. Nor did I often hear the subject raised in the church as I was growing up.

That night before I went to bed, I asked my mother how I could be saved. She very eagerly, but lovingly and sensitively, told me the salvation story and how I could invite Jesus to come into my heart. I said a little prayer and did just that. I asked her if that meant that I was saved now. She said that I was. I asked her if it meant that if she and my father were taken to heaven I would be taken too. She said that it did. I then began to worry about my little sister and brother. It wasn't long before they were both saved too.

A few years later, I was baptized and accepted into the fellowship of Dunning Park Chapel. Each of my decisions— to be saved, to be baptized, to enter into the fellowship of the church—were met with great approval and tremendous affirmation by my parents, friends, and the people of the church. I was off to a great Christian start, and it was clear to all that this boy was going places.

One of the things I learned early was that the Plymouth Brethren Church had the truth; we were closest to what the New Testament really taught. The Baptists were the next closest, the Methodists were okay. But among the Presbyterians, Episcopalians, and Lutherans things were pretty shaky. And of course we all knew that Catholics weren't really Christians. There were always new converts in our church who "used to be Catholic."

I grew up believing that I was part of the best family in the best church in the best state in the best country in the whole world. Until I was thirteen.

At thirteen, the world I had grown up in went sour on me. All the ideas and interests into which I had poured my energy and time began to lose their attraction.

My life no longer felt exciting or satisfying, and I became restless. Before long I became rebellious. In some ways, mine was a typical adolescent rebellion, but it hit harder than most and had long-lasting consequences.

The families of my old neighborhood, as they became more financially secure, tended to move away, as we did when I reached junior high school. The move my family made that year underscored the feeling that I was entering a new stage in my life. It was a move up—to the upper middle class and a suburb of Detroit called Southfield. Southfield was only ten miles from where I had grown up, but it was a different world. The church was the only carry-over from life in Redford Township.

As a result of my father's promotions and raises and the miracle of installment buying, we began to change our life-style. We built a much larger house on a much larger lot, doing a great deal of work ourselves with the help of friends from the church.

More room to play, ball fields all around, our own bedrooms, and maybe some day a swimming pool were enticements my parents described to us before the move. Except for the pool, it all came true. But I never did like the new neighborhood or school as well as the old ones.

I became alienated, critical, unhappy—and cynical about all the values, institutions, and people who had once held authority for me. In the space of a few months I quit organized sports, dropped off the honor roll, and earned a "D" in spelling. (My mother rightly pointed out that as such a good speller I had to have tried hard to get such a grade.)

With all the difficult merit badges behind me, I had been on my way to becoming one of the youngest Eagle Scouts in the city of Detroit. Much to my father's diappointment, I gave it up. Perhaps it was prophetic that one merit badge I failed to get was "Citizenship in the Nation."

I taunted my teachers in the new school, deliberately missing their easy questions, which I thought were insulting, and then answering the most difficult ones. I went from being everyone's favorite son to a disrespectful kid who was a behavior problem.

It was the beginning of a serious confrontation with my parents, my father in particular. I had gone from model son to uncontrollable teen-ager almost overnight. My mother has said to me in recent years, "We had you until you were thirteen, and then we never had control of you again."

Before long I started wearing tight pants and pointed shoes. My "brushcut" hairstyle was grown out into a "waterfall." My mother wondered what had happened to her fair-haired boy who now went through a tube of Brylcreem every two weeks. She often told me I looked terrible; she was probably right. My father especially hated my long hair, as it symbolized to him my rebellion.

My music was another issue. Until that time, only soundtracks from musicals like *South Pacific, Oklahoma,* and *My Fair Lady,* and hymns by George Beverly Shea, Billy Graham's soloist, were heard in our home. It was a big jump to Dion, Del Shannon, and the rest of the rock and roll I became absorbed in. These were the early years of Motown. The Supremes, the Temptations, Smokey Robinson and the Miracles, and Little Stevie Wonder were all local talent for big high school dances. Motown got into my blood.

I went to parties every Friday and Saturday night and often in between. I discovered I loved to dance, one of the taboos of my Plymouth Brethren Church. The twist was big in those days.

I became what was known in Detroit in the early 1960s as a "hood," which was a very cool thing to be at that time in the city of fast cars. I thought the girls were especially cool, wearing microscopic skirts and black stockings, pale makeup accentuated with white lipstick, and teasing their hair enough to rival any sparrow's nest.

I really wanted to be tough, but I wasn't very big and I had a baby face; all the scowls in the world wouldn't cover that up. I never actually got into any serious trouble, nor did I smoke or drink like most of my friends.

But I did have a bad reputation. This was of course a big problem in the church. The preacher's kid, the one most likely to succeed, the one who would "be a leader of this church someday," had become a hood. A few years ago, when I went back to visit the church, some of the elders told me that they had in those days and for several years thereafter warned their children to stay away from me. I looked like everything the elders were preaching against. When they talked about young people going wrong, I was there as a constant reminder of just how bad kids could get.

My rebellious life-style brought some momentary satisfaction, but I eventually grew tired of it. My restlessness went deeper, and I knew it wasn't going to be solved by long hair, tight pants, and being cool. I was disillusioned with it all, but I still had no desire to be a good and obedient son.

Eventually I got a haircut, let the seams out of my pants, took the points off my shoes, and stopped going to all the parties. I grew increasingly introverted, retreating into my thoughts and unanswered questions.

My only real reinvolvement with school was in choral music, which was always a great love. Two highlights of my high school career were the solo "Maria" from *West Side Story*, which I sang, and a kilt scene in *Brigadoon*. My grades rose again, but I never found my studies challenging or stimulating. Student government seemed patronizing and irrelevant.

My love for sports never left me, but the competition, machismo, obedience to authority, and team spirit that bordered on the militaristic, felt oppressive to me. I never became a varsity athlete, and I wasn't interested in the clubs.

My mind was filled with questions I couldn't answer. I had a deep sense that something was terribly wrong—with my world, my country, and my church. And I began to realize that it had something to do with the condition of black people.

2
The First Contradiction: Racism

In the summer of 1967, Detroit exploded into a city at war with itself. For years it had been a tinderbox of racial hatred, and an incident between black residents and white police finally ignited the resentment, hurt, and anger.

I remember vividly the terrible fear that the riots created in white people. Afraid that blacks would break out of the ghetto to attack and burn the suburbs, the police and armed, white vigilante groups stood guard at the borders of suburban communities.

To anyone who had any understanding of the conditions under which blacks lived in Detroit, the riots were predictable. The white response to them could also have been foretold, as the vigilante groups were merely a visible manifestation of an attitude that ran deep.

Detroit in the 1960s was two communities, one white and one black, separate and dramatically unequal. Growing up white in Detroit, I had no exposure to black people, but for an occasional glimpse on a downtown bus or at a Tigers baseball game. What I was told about them was based on the stereotypes so common to white culture.

I knew only that blacks lived in the inner city (a bad place to live), were the poorest people in Detroit, had the worst jobs or none at all, and filled the city's jails. I felt the tension and hostility that pervaded the conversations among whites whenever the subject of blacks, race, the city, or crime came up; people whom I knew to be otherwise kind and loving would be transformed, uttering vicious words of intolerance and fearful hatred.

I wanted to know why. My growing alienation and questioning began to focus on one overriding issue: the status of black people in America.

Why did whites and blacks live completely divided from one another? Why were whites rich and blacks poor? What created the fear? I was persistent in taking my questions to my parents, teachers, and friends, but I soon discovered that no one could answer them. Some simply evaded the questions. Others told me that I was too young to be concerned about such things and that someday I would understand.

Hoping that the church might provide some answers, I asked: "What about our Christian faith? Doesn't God love all people?" I reminded the people of the church of a song I was taught as a child in Sunday school: "Jesus loves the little children,/All the children of the world;/Red and yellow, black and white,/They are precious in His sight;/Jesus loves the little children of the world."

Of course the song is true and God loves everybody, I was told, but there are differences. And of course we love everybody too, but that doesn't mean we have to live together.

I asked the church people why we sent missionaries to Africa but didn't have any contact with black people in our own city. Weren't there a lot of black Christians, and why didn't our churches ever have anything to do with one another?

I was told that we were better off separated. Some even used the Bible to undergird their argument, citing the Genesis story in which Noah curses the descendants of his son Ham.

Others said that blacks were happy with the way things were. They had their ways and places to live, and we had ours. There should be no problems. And if they had problems, they probably deserved them; after all, they were lazy, had too many children, and were dangerous.

Some people told me that asking these questions would only get me into trouble. That proved to be the only honest answer I ever got.

It didn't take long for me to realize that I wasn't going to get the answers I was looking for from white people. So I decided to make my way into the inner city.

The first thing I discovered, to my great surprise, was that there were black Plymouth Brethren assemblies in inner-city Detroit. They were just like my church in most ways, right down to the same dreadful hymnbook, and I wondered why I had never been told about them. I sought out the elders of the black churches and learned that they had known about our assemblies for years. Most even recognized my name because of the role my father played in the Detroit assemblies, and some had even met him.

As I asked my questions, a new world opened up. Here were black church leaders making time in their very busy lives for a young white kid, full of questions, who had come to see them in the inner city. They were extraordinarily patient and receptive, never patronizing and always compassionate. They must have been smiling inside at my idealism and the questions that had such obvious answers to them, but they never let on.

I felt that the church should lead the way toward change. One of my first ideas was that we get our churches together and march through the streets of Detroit on behalf of racial justice. They wisely suggested we start smaller.

I believed that if black and white Christians would simply pray and examine the Bible together, they would learn to love one another and begin to change. I was excited at the prospect. We decided on some meetings with people in the white churches. I learned later that the black leaders had been through all this before.

I'm sure I was so aggressive in setting up the meetings that the white Christians didn't know what to do except go along with the scheme. I will never forget our first get-together—in a white church, of course, since my white friends weren't about to go into the inner city. I can still see the polite, frozen smiles on their faces as they awkwardly shook hands with my new black friends.

There were not many meetings, and the idea soon died out. The interest was always strong from the black Christians, though I'm not sure why they were still willing to try after all the abuse they had received from white Christians. They were open and very reconciling in their posture. There were no angry words or militant spirits from these gracious saints.

My favorite was Bill Pannell. Bill was a young leader in the black Plymouth Brethren assemblies, a fine Bible teacher and preacher with a growing ministry. I had heard from older, white evangelicals that he was an angry militant, a radical. He had a bad reputation among some white churches, but by then I knew something about bad reputations.

I was deeply touched by reading Bill's book, *My Friend, the Enemy,* a painful and articulate account of the experience of growing up black in white America. I felt especially hurt by his recounting of the racism in white churches.

Bill's photograph was on the back cover of the book. With his picture in hand, I went to a church where he was scheduled to speak and, after his talk, approached him and awkwardly introduced myself. I tried to explain why I wanted to talk with him. From the first, he was willing and eager.

I recognized Bill Pannell as a man with fire in his eyes because of the flame that glowed deep within his heart. He had grown up around white Christians and he knew them well, but his heart burned with compassion for his own people. He was warm, sensitive, very insightful, and deeply passionate—the kind of Christian I wanted to be. He also had a great sense of humor and loved to laugh.

Bill was able to answer more of my questions than anyone else. Listening to him made many things come into focus for me. He offered the kind of clarification of thought and spiritual direction that I was never able to find in the white assemblies. At a time when I didn't have much respect for authority, Bill's authority quickly commended itself to me.

Today Bill's stature in the broader Christian community continues to grow. He is now professor of evangelism at Fuller

Theological Seminary in Pasadena, California, chairman of the board of Youth for Christ International, a well-respected speaker and writer, and a leader in the black community who has had a strong impact on the white evangelical world.

My respect and affection for Bill have grown over the years, and I am honored to have him as a contributing editor for *Sojourners*. After almost twenty years, and many changes in my life, Bill Pannell is still a faithful friend. At a formative time, he helped set my feet on the right path, and for that I will always be grateful.

Bill's was not the only book I read. I devoured everything I could get my hands on written by or about black people and racism in America. The simple, self-justifying world view of my childhood and my church, conflicting with my growing awareness of racism and poverty, caused mounting havoc in my teen-age years. I was shocked at what I read, felt betrayed and angry at the brutal facts of racism. Worse, I felt painfully implicated.

The Autobiography of Malcolm X became one of the most influential books on my life. Malcolm's personal account tells the story of black people in America better than anything else I have read. Especially startling to me was the part of Malcolm's life that took place in my home state of Michigan. Many places where he had lived were names with which I was familiar, including Lansing, where I later attended Michigan State University. Though he was never accepted by the white community, Malcolm was truly one of the great black leaders in America's history.

Charles Silberman's *Crisis in Black and White* was another such book. It was assigned reading in an expository writing class taught by Mrs. Susan Wallendorf, a high school English teacher and radical in her own way. The book enlightened me and utterly convinced me of the depth and breadth of racism in America.

I was sure that it would have the same effect on my classmates, but I was proven entirely wrong in our class discussion about the book. Only Mrs. Wallendorf and I were sympathetic to the book's perspective. The others responded with a defensiveness and hostility toward black people that left me stunned.

Mrs. Wallendorf probably never knew the effect that she and her English class had on me. She also had us read *Hiroshima* by John Hersey, the story of the victims of the first atomic bombing. I could not know then how nuclear weaponry would eventually become as overriding an issue in my life as that of racism.

As my commitment to the struggle for racial justice intensified, I wanted to go further in my relationship with the black community. I desired to go beyond the black church and become schooled in those streams of black thought and action that were more militant and radical.

I began to seek opportunities for interaction and dialogue, especially with young black workers and students. Over several summers I took jobs working first as a machine operator in a small factory and then on custodial and maintenance crews in Detroit office buildings. The blacks I met were much more angry and bitter than the black Christians I had come to know, and they provided me with a new education.

They were Detroit's manual laborers and unskilled workers, who slaved hard for little money. They had no future in the system, and they knew it. The goods of a consumer society were dangled in front of their eyes like carrots on a stick, but they were systematically shut out of the good life.

They never had the opportunity for a decent education. They lived in upstairs flats, rooming houses, ghetto apartments overflowing with parents, brothers and sisters, grandparents, and friends who had no other place to stay. Many were at home on the streets and had become tough at an early age in order to survive.

Butch was typical of the young, bright members of Detroit's urban poor. Butch and I worked together as janitors at Detroit Edison the summer before I went to college. Our lives were as different as the destinations of our paychecks. Mine went into a savings account for college, and none of it had to go for room and board since I was still living at home during the summer. His went to support his wife, mother, and all his sisters and brothers, who lived together in a small place in one of Detroit's worst neighborhoods.

According to the executives and their secretaries at Detroit Edison, the difference in the color of our skin meant Butch and I merited different treatment. Their race and class bias was blatant. I was often put on moving crews with Butch and the other blacks who worked there. They were regarded at best as men with strong backs and no heads, and at worst as beasts of burden. Nineteen-year-old office secretaries ordered them around, complaining constantly about their work.

The resentment among the custodial crew went very deep. After a while, some of them trusted me enough to talk openly in my presence about the hatred they felt for the system and those who ran it.

Butch and I were often put on elevator duty together. We both had to endure an insufferable barrage of bad jokes from the upper echelon workers such as, "Bet this job has its ups and downs," and, "You're moving up faster than anyone in this whole company." We had been instructed to be polite and humor the people. But I never had to suffer the patronizing tone which always greeted Butch. I received respect because it was known that I was soon to be a university student and had every opportunity to be one of them one day.

The job became a school in political understanding, and Butch was a ready commentator and tutor. One night when we were working late, we were asked to clean the executive offices on the fifth floor. These offices of the company president, the chairman of the board, all the vice presidents and executive officers, were more than extravagant. As I took in every inch of the spacious offices and conference rooms with thick pile rugs, hardwood furniture, and expensive art, Butch said, "Come here, I want to show you something." Well hidden away were the executive liquor cabinets, stocked full of the finest liquors and wines money could buy. Butch commented, "You think these guys spend all their time up here working, huh?"

I was never more ashamed at the abuses of power and wealth. Butch was struggling to survive and could never have dreamed of tasting such opulence. I was beginning to see that to stand with those who suffered I would have to shed myself of the assumptions of privilege and comfort on which I had been raised.

Butch was very savvy—about the streets, the job, Detroit, and international politics. His education came from the pages of the perpetual string of books he kept tucked in the back pocket of his khaki janitor's uniform. His experience of oppression and his reflections on it were turning him into a political revolutionary. He was very conscious of and committed to the worldwide black liberation struggle, and he knew as much about African history as I did about American. My growing political awareness was bringing my convictions in line with his.

The job gave us an opportunity to spend literally hours together. We had many of our best conversations in the elevators. Elevator operators are required by law to get periodic breaks, as going up and down all day without a respite begins to make one's head spin. But mine was already reeling with all the thoughts and ideas Butch was helping nurture along, so I spent all my breaks in his elevator, and he spent his in mine.

We must have appeared as quite a startling pair to the office workers, toward whom we eventually learned to be oblivious as we continued our conversations nonstop while carrying them up and down. Here were two young men, one black and one white, carrying on intense conversations about revolution, urban guerrilla warfare in Detroit, and the overthrow of the capitalist system, while taking middle-management executives to their third-floor offices.

Butch and I talked about everything: our backgrounds, our families and neighborhoods, our churches. We discussed black consciousness, the police, and the suburbs. Though we lived in the same city, we might as well have grown up in two different countries.

Violence, both on the streets and in corporate board-rooms, was a continuing conversation. He gave me his views on the war in Vietnam as an imperialist war against people of color in which he would refuse to fight.

Eventually, Butch invited me to come to his home and meet his family. I felt deeply honored and very eager to go. But every time I asked him to write directions to his place, he would change the subject. Finally one day with pen and paper in hand, I sat him down and said, "Look, Butch, how do you expect me to get to your house if you don't write out directions for me?"

Awkwardly he began to scribble on the paper. I was deeply sad when I realized the reason he had hesitated before was that he could barely write; I was ashamed of my insensitivity.

That small incident was very significant to me. I went home that night and both cried and cursed. I could not believe that someone as bright as Butch had hardly been taught to write. I was furious at a system that had given me so much and him almost nothing, simply by virtue of our skin color. By accident of birth, I had all the benefits and he all the suffering. I vowed again through angry tears to do everything I could to change that system.

On the appointed evening, I went to Butch's house. I attracted a good bit of attention driving into his neighborhood and getting out of the car; in those days, white people didn't venture into certain neighborhoods of Detroit.

All but Butch's youngest brothers and sisters were nervous and suspicious of what a white man was doing in their home. The older they were, the deeper were the hurt and distrust in their eyes. But almost from the moment I sat down, the youngest ones were in my lap, smiling, their bright eyes sparkling at a new-found friend.

That experience has been repeated many times since. One can be overwhelmed by the spontaneity and affection of young black children. Those responses can be easily mistaken as a sign of racial reconciliation rather than what they are: an expression of beautiful innocence. It doesn't take long for ghetto life, the streets, and experience with white people to turn that innocence into bitterness and despair.

I stayed for several hours. When the older ones realized that I really was a friend to Butch, they began to open up. That too is a common experience.

I was especially taken by Butch's mother. She was a lovely woman, gracious and warm, so anxious for me to feel at home. She was just like my mother in so many ways. She wasn't interested in politics, was certainly not militant, would never have been taken for a radical. She was primarily concerned about the same things my mother was: the health, happiness, and safety of her family.

Her love for Butch was obvious. Since she had lost her husband, Butch had filled his shoes as the family provider. As the eldest son, he was her pride and joy. Butch's love and respect for his mother was also evident.

But I could also see how fearful she was of his growing anger and militance. She, just like my mother, was afraid that her son's political views would get him into trouble. It wasn't that she disagreed with him, but that she was afraid he might be hurt.

I asked her questions about her past, her experiences in Detroit, her family. She had a way of looking into your eyes and speaking right to your heart. I knew that I was hearing the honest reflections of a proud woman who had somehow kept her family together through the difficulties of growing up black in Detroit.

She recounted a history of poverty and abuse. I will never forget what she said about the police. She told of countless times that her husband or one of her sons had been picked up on the street for no apparent reason, taken down to the precinct, falsely accused, verbally abused, and even beaten.

She would go down every time to find out what had happened and try to bring them home. Each time she was assaulted with vile and profane language. The police would tell her that they would "take care of" her husband or son, give her man what he deserved, and that she'd better "get her ass on home" or she was going to get the same treatment.

My insides began to hurt and my eyes to well up with tears as one by one every person in the room told me stories of how they or close friends had been abused by the police, mostly for the crime of being at the wrong place at the wrong time and being black. I knew then that the reputation that the Detroit police had for brutalizing black people had been earned.

The image I had of the police as I was growing up came to my mind. My mother had told us kids that if we ever got lost, we should try to find a policeman, and he would help us and bring us home. Butch's mother told her kids that if they were ever lost and couldn't find their way home, they should try to avoid the police because if the police found them, they might hurt them. The police were known for verbally and physically abusing black children if they wandered too far from home.

There are many more people whom I came to know and stories that could be told from those years. The fact is that people like Butch and his family were my teachers. If education is to learn to see the truth, to know the world as it really is, then my education began when I got to know black people in Detroit.

They showed me the other America, the America that is unfair and wrong and mean and hateful; the America that we white people accept. But they taught me about more than racism. They taught me about love and family and courage, about what is most important and what it means to be a human being. By listening to the black experience, I discovered more truth about myself, my country, and my faith than by listening anywhere else.

I became preoccupied with the role of black people in America. I wondered if they were placed here by God to teach America the truth about itself. It seemed to me that black people were central for America's salvation. Certainly the black community had become crucial to mine.

In light of the pervasiveness of white racism, I still don't understand why so many people in the black community were so good to me. They took me in. They treated me like a friend and allowed me to see the world a bit through their eyes. They listened to my naïve questions and responded to them with the only answers that ever made sense to me.

When those questions were finally answered, I felt a deep sense of betrayal by white America. I was disillusioned with my country and my upbringing as never before. My burning question became, Why hadn't I been told?

White America successfully kept the truth hidden, kept itself isolated and protected, until the truth finally could no longer stay ghetto-ized. It blew up in the faces of white America in cities around the country in the late 1960s.

The black anger that tore Detroit apart created not so much a riot as an insurrection. At root it was a political rebellion against the oppression and control of white America. Some of the young black men who tore up the city of Detroit in the summer of 1967 were friends of mine. I talked with them before and after, and I knew that their motives had more to do with political rebellion than random violence.

The riots were an explosion of pent-up rage, and the weight of oppression was their cause. Black political leaders went to the streets and tried in vain to quell the crowds, but it was too late. A revolutionary spirit had taken over, and nothing anyone could do or say would stop it.

The result was many people killed, countless more injured, and millions of dollars of property damage. The official death count was forty-three, but everyone knew that more people were killed than was ever reported by the media.

Most of the casualties were black. I heard of incidents of black men lynched by white police and citizens, of black women being hauled into precinct houses and gang-raped by white police. The blacks fought back.

Black snipers shot and killed white police. A few white motorists who happened to be at the wrong place at the wrong time were dragged from their cars, beaten and killed. Windows were smashed, stores looted, businesses—black and white alike—destroyed. Whole sections of the city went up in flames.

The city just stopped. Business as usual halted. I never saw anything like it before or since. People were afraid to go out of their houses, especially at night, and a curfew was soon placed over the city.

The police started to lose control, and the National Guard were sent into the streets with rifles, gas masks, and tanks, like an occupying army moving into the ghetto. It was like a class war, a colonial situation in which the white ruling group was being threatened by a popular uprising.

Pitched rifle battles took place between the Guard and the snipers, the sort of urban guerrilla warfare Butch and I had talked about while going up and down in our elevators. I recall that right after the riots, Butch started carrying in his pocket a book called *The Race War*, which called for open, armed struggle against the white community.

One night a local Detroit sportscaster almost in tears stopped right in the middle of his sportscast and, with his voice cracking, said he couldn't go on: "How can I talk about sports when our city is destroying itself? I just don't have anything to say."

I remember wanting to go into the riot areas during the rebellion, but I would never have gotten in and to try would have been foolish. The ghetto was cordoned off as in a military operation, with police barricades and a strict curfew. I maintained an almost around-the-clock vigil at the television or radio, watching and listening to what was happening just a few miles away.

I could get close enough to see the flames at night. They lit the sky up brightly, and it looked as though the whole ghetto was burning down. I could hear gunshots and sirens, and I wondered what was happening to the people I knew. I felt angry and helpless.

Virtually all the white people I talked to blamed the rioting on black people. The riots were totally baffling and deeply frightening to them. I felt helplessly stuck in the middle, unable to get into the city, unable to relate to the fear and lack of understanding expressed by my white friends and neighbors.

When the riots were over, my father and I drove into the city to survey the scene, which looked literally like a war zone. Gutted buildings, abandoned storefronts, piles of rubble—Detroit looked like it had been bombed. Soldiers still patrolled the streets, giving the scene a feel of martial law, which was in fact what the situation had become.

Later the *Kerner Report,* the presidential commission study of the riots in Detroit, Newark, and other U.S. cities, identified their cause as the white racism that divided our society against itself. I must have read that report at least five times, studying its more than six-hundred pages with a thorough intensity. It completely confirmed my experience of the black community. The causes of urban violence were poverty and its accompanying miseries: bad housing and inadequate education, lack of medical care, high unemployment. And the most commonly mentioned grievance by all the black people surveyed was police brutality.

For a long time I had tried to get my church to deal with the issue of racism. After the riots, the people of the church finally agreed to take up the subject. Even then it was relegated to a Wednesday night midweek meeting rather than Sunday morning.

The format of the meeting was to be a panel discussion, and I was to take "the side of the blacks." Two of the church's elders were selected to take the other side, the "white point of view." The fourth panelist was a young social worker new to the church, who was sympathetic to the black perspective.

I never prepared harder for anything in my life. My presentation was chock-full of unemployment figures, housing statistics, facts about poverty, welfare, inadequate education and health care, police brutality. It was also overflowing with Bible verses that dealt with God's love for the poor and concern for justice, and the reconciling work of Christ.

By the time the big night came I knew I was ready. I was sure that no one could dispute the facts of the situation or disagree with the overwhelming biblical imperatives for justice and racial reconciliation. I began my remarks with a line from a song by a black Detroit singer, which spoke to the depth of her personal despair: "The windows of the world are covered with rain; what's the whole thing coming to?" I shared what I had learned from blacks about their experiences of being poor, segregated, and disenfranchised. The social worker buttressed my argument with more facts and stories from his experience in social work.

The response from the two elders was predictable. One spoke of how his Scottish grandparents had pulled themselves up from their bootstraps as immigrants to America, and he asked why blacks couldn't do the same. The other spent his time defending the American way of life, praising the virtues of capitalism. They failed completely to engage with anything I had said.

The discussion was then opened up to the congregation, and I hoped the conversation would improve. The first question set the tone for the evening. One of the adults who had known me since birth directed his question to me, "But, Jamie, would you really want Barbie (my younger sister) to marry one?"

It got worse from there. Most people refused to look at the suffering of black people. One after another they rose to emotionally defend themselves, their church, white America, and its way of life.

By the end of the evening I was thoroughly discouraged. Only my parents and the wife of the young social worker expressed any real support. People who had known me all my life came up to me afterward and offered a string of empty, patronizing remarks about how impressed they were with my presentation.

My first idealistic impulses had driven me to take my concerns to the church, with the hope that the church members would respond. Their defensive reaction and opposition to me only spawned greater awareness and more action, which spawned more reaction, and—it's a familiar story.

As the church people sought to justify themselves and the country they loved, that country seemed uglier and uglier to me. Even my parents, who had always taken a firm stand against any personal expression of racist attitudes by their friends and supported my raising the issue in the church, began to grow afraid and confused by my increasing alienation.

That alienation from the church over the issue of racism grew to anger when I went away to college. I had little to do with the church after I went away, but occasionally when I was home for a weekend, at the persuasion of my parents, I paid a visit on Sunday morning.

I remember one Sunday when the preacher was a white missionary to South Africa. He gave a rather contentless devotional talk that said nothing about the situation of apartheid in South Africa.

Afterwards I walked up to him to have a few words. One of the church elders, who was waiting to take him home for Sunday dinner, saw me coming. Worry was written all over the elder's face.

I asked our speaker what American missionaries were doing to oppose the racially segregated and exploitative system of apartheid in South Africa. He smiled and whispered, "Now I know that in this country you have a belief in integration. But let me tell you that it would never work in South Africa. We know these people and, believe me, we love these people, but they just couldn't handle equality with whites. The whites are the only ones who can really run the country, and the blacks and the coloreds are better off with apartheid than they would be without it. I know because I've been there."

Quite sure of himself, he was a bit unprepared for my response and astonished by it. I looked at him with all the anger and bitterness that had been growing inside me for a long time toward such hypocrisy, and I said, "Some day when black people in South Africa rise up to take their freedom and put people like you up against the wall, don't you dare have the gall to say that you are being persecuted for the sake of Christ."

The missionary stood dazed for a moment with his mouth gaping, while the church elder turned so red I thought he might burst. Being an evangelist and assuming from my remark that I couldn't be a Christian, the missionary asked me if I had ever been to the church before. I replied that I had been there all my life and was now away at college. A smile of understanding crept over his face, and he nodded, "Oh, I see, you're away at college. One of those secular schools, no doubt."

Such interactions were typical of those years in my life. I had become a very angry young man, especially about the hypocrisy of the church. Little gentleness or humility could be found in my rage, and I'm sure I was more than just a little self-righteous and arrogant.

The people of the church and I found ourselves less and less able to talk with one another, and none of us had much desire or energy for it anymore. I continued to drift farther and farther away from Christian faith.

Finally, the alienation from the church that my confrontation with racism had begun was completed by Vietnam.

3
The Second Contradiction: The War

"We are all outlaws in the eyes of America." This line from a song by the Jefferson Airplane, popular in the late 1960s, became dear to the student antiwar movement. At Michigan State University, I found a home among the other outlaws.

The brutal facts of racism had already shattered the comfortable world view of my evangelical upbringing. By the time the war in Vietnam erupted in the American consciousness, I was no longer innocent in regard to the contradictions between America's ideals and its practice. Black Detroit had unlocked the door to new understanding, and Vietnam threw the door wide open. The oppression of the poor was not only a problem within the borders of America, but was the key to understanding U.S. policy abroad.

The black experience in Detroit had made me suspicious of official pronouncements, and I was inclined to disbelieve the things the government said about its role in Vietnam. That suspicion was shared among several of the students with whom I came into contact at MSU in 1966.

Many of my generation made it our business to find out the truth about Vietnam. The war became our tutor.

My friends and I spent endless hours studying Vietnamese history, culture, and politics. We tried to probe behind our government's veil of secrecy and official deception and worked hard at uncovering the roots and reasons for the war. We discovered that the American involvement in Vietnam was not an aberration, but in fact only the most current example of a long and bloody record of U.S. interventionism, especially in nations of the Third World.

At the heart of this ugly record has been economic and political self-interest. Our country has a history of backing dictators with little regard for the way they treat their own people. Like former colonial powers, we have backed wealthy elites who sacrifice national self-determination for personal aggrandizement. I remembered being told while growing up that this was the way of communist Russia, but that America was different.

And I had believed that America was different. So had the other leaders of the radical student movement. We were America's most idealistic children. Like me, most were well educated, the products of middle-class homes, would-be heirs of the fruits of affluence and privilege. Many were former student government leaders, some had also been youth group leaders in their churches, and the number of Eagle Scouts in our ranks would have embarrassed the national Scout organization.

We had made the mistake of believing in America. Eventually, we learned that our faith had been misplaced. Underneath the anger of young student radicals (which was always the characteristic given the most publicity) was a deep well of hurt and disillusionment, and a feeling of betrayal.

We committed the unpardonable sin: we said that America was wrong—wrong in the ghettos and in the jungles of Southeast Asia. And for our opposition we were regarded as criminals.

When the idealism and talent of youth were turned against the system, that system turned against us, and it began to number student protesters among its enemies. We were no longer America's promising children, but "leftists" and "communist sympathizers," or, as Richard Nixon was fond of calling us, "bums." Whatever vestiges of idealism about America that we still may have clung to were quickly gone as we became even more sobered by the response we received to our protest.

I remember an incident that took place during the national student strike in the spring of 1970. The strike had been called in response to the U.S. invasion of Cambodia and the killing of four students by the National Guard at Kent State University.

I was one of the elected strike leaders at Michigan State. One night, with a couple hundred other students in the student union building, which had often been a rallying point for the movement, I was preparing for teach-ins that were to take place the next day. At closing time, with still a great deal of work to do, we decided to occupy the building through the night—both as a show of strength to the university and because we needed a place to finish our preparations for the next day's teachings on the war.

We called the university administration to assure them that we would be out by morning, as well as to promise that there would be no property damage; they had worked with us long enough to know that our word was good on such things. We informed them that we were not looking for a confrontation and that it would do no one any good to provoke one.

At about three in the morning, I went for a walk with a few friends, other strike leaders. We were gone only fifteen minutes, but when we returned the student union was completely encircled by police from three adjoining counties. Everyone within the circle was under arrest and everyone outside the building was prevented from entering.

The leaders of the police raid were angry when we appeared behind them and they realized we had slipped through their net. Later the university admitted that their plan had been to arrest and jail all the strike leaders and thereby end the strike. The authorities always had the mistaken idea that the antiwar movement was the product of a few hardcore radicals and outside agitators, and if these could be rounded up, the rest of the students would go back to swallowing goldfish and carrying off pantie raids.

By four in the morning the police had begun to process on the street more than a hundred students, who that night received criminal records. I stood on the edge of the police barricade shouting information to the students being arrested about what they should and should not submit to, both to give support and to make the police aware that they were being watched and must be respectful of the students' civil rights.

A crowd began to gather to watch the arrest scene. Being a former youth group song leader, I began to lead the students, both those being arrested and those observing, in choruses of patriotic medleys. It was truly a great scene: youthful, white students being fingerprinted, photographed for mug shots, handcuffed, and put into waiting MSU buses, all joining in unison to sing "The Star-Spangled Banner," "America the Beautiful," and "My country, 'tis of thee,/Sweet land of liberty." I always knew that my Christian training would be useful in the movement some day.

The following day one of the other strike leaders strode right past the secretaries in the dean of students' office to say to the startled dean, "Thank you, thank you, for making a hundred students into revolutionaries!"

I think that something important happens to each of us the first time we are confronted by the police, arrested, or put in jail. We are raised to believe that the law exists to protect and serve us, to defend our interests and secure our futures. Police wagons, courts, and jails are filled with people who are different from us, people in trouble with the law who must have done something wrong to deserve punishment.

It is a great shock for the average middle-class kid to suddenly find himself or herself on the wrong side of the law. It fundamentally transforms one's self-consciousness. You begin to see that the law is on the side of racism and war, and that law and order are often code words for the suppression of dissent and the frustration of social change.

To be counted as criminals for the sake of political conscience is the beginning of a taste of what for years has been the experience of poor, black, and Third-World people—anyone who ends up on the wrong side of the interests of American wealth and power. White America's children were getting an inkling of what blacks had been dealt for years.

The change did not come easy at first. I had been raised to fear "radicals." I remember well the day I realized that I was one of them, which simply meant that I was opposed to my country's perpetuation of racism, poverty, and war. My community, and in many ways my family, became those who were struggling for civil rights and an end to the war in Vietnam. I found a new home in the movement, with those students who, like me, were alienated and were seeking to bring about fundamental social change while searching out alternatives for their own lives. I had joined the other side.

I was at Michigan State University from 1966 to 1970, at the height of the Vietnam War protest. In those years, trying to stop the war was more important than anything else. Especially for the leaders of the movement, antiwar activity took precedence over both our formal studies and our social life. We were majoring in trying to stop the war.

The war galvanized student opinion across the campus. During the student strike, for example, thousands of students participated in a campus-wide election for a strike steering committee.

A meeting was called in the MSU auditorium a few days later to hammer out democratically what our demands to the administration would be. More than ten thousand students came and sat through six hours of discussion; no more than three thousand had ever voted in a student government election.

For hours, students lined up behind microphones and debated each proposal. Every demand had to receive majority approval, and the strike leadership made sure that every point of view had an opportunity to be expressed. It was the most democratic process I had ever been a part of.

It was an exciting time to be at the university. Virtually every night on the CBS *Evening News,* Walter Cronkite reported more protest on one campus or another. Universities were no longer cloistered academic communities removed from the turmoil of the world; they were in the thick of the political struggles that dominated the times.

A revolutionary spirit pervaded it all for us. During the height of the student strike, the stock market began to plummet, and we were elated.

The administration of MSU accused the student leaders of making the university political. Our response was that the university had made itself political by its involvement in U.S. foreign policy and war-making.

Michigan State was deeply implicated in the war. The university had a long association with the CIA. John Hannah, the president of MSU when I entered, eventually retired to take up the post as head of AID, an organization known to be closely associated with the CIA. His replacement, Clifton Wharton, came to Michigan State via the Rockefeller Foundation. One of the early lessons of our political education was that in American establishment politics, the top positions are all kept in the family and are passed out as rewards for a job well done.

Ngo Dinh Diem, one of South Vietnam's military dictators during that period, had been personally recruited by Wesley Fischel, a political science professor at MSU. Members of Diem's secret police were trained by the MSU Department of Public Safety. Down the road at the University of Michigan, major research was being done for the Department of Defense.

The records of Michigan State's involvement with the war effort have since been purged from the university's computer. But the sordid story was well known to the antiwar movement and became part of the "alternative orientation" we ran for incoming freshmen every year.

During the most intense antiwar activity, the campus was filled with police and security officers. Some days it seemed like an armed camp. During the 1970 student strike, more than two hundred plainclothes police were on MSU's campus, from local undercover police to FBI agents—the locals were those who looked like high school basketball coaches leaning against red Ford Mustangs.

I cannot remember the number of times I was tear-gassed and chased by police with clubs. My phone was tapped. I was under surveillance, sometimes followed. There were periods of time when I never went for a walk or a ride without periodically looking over my shoulder.

I was both lied to and harassed by university and police authorities. Because of my political activity, the administration threatened several times to relieve me of my position as resident adviser in my dormitory, which I held for three of my four years at MSU. It was also common for student antiwar leaders to be threatened with expulsion from school. Members of the university administration informed us that there were security files on us both in Michigan and Washington that could prevent us from getting good jobs or entering graduate school.

Private citizens and local vigilante groups also tried to intimidate student protesters. Occasionally strange voices would call in the middle of the night with threats of physical violence. Sometimes such violence was carried out.

In the spring of 1970, more than ten thousand people marched to the state capitol in downtown Lansing. It was at the height of popular sentiment against the war, and all along the route people waved and smiled in support of our demonstration and in opposition to U.S. policy in Vietnam.

It was a perfect spring day, beautifully sunny. Our marshalls were well-trained, in position, and controlling the crowd easily. Our police escort was very cooperative. I had no responsibilities until we arrived downtown, and I was enjoying the leisurely march in the company of a few friends.

Suddenly, people in front of us began to scream, turn, and run. A car coming down the other side of the street had veered sharply into the crowd. I could see bodies flying in every direction and people diving to get out of the way of the oncoming automobile. I literally picked up the friend on my right, who was almost blind, and threw him out of the path of the car. Another friend and I dove out of the way as the car continued through the fear-struck crowd, finally coming to a stop when it hit a large curb.

People had been mowed down and were strewn on the

ground in the car's path, some screaming and calling out in pain. First-aid attendants had already begun to take care of the injured. The scene was chaos and panic, as people milled about in fear and anger. We were in the middle of the downtown shopping district, and literally anything could have happened.

The crowd converged on the car, and people began to pound on it. Though as angry as the others, I was fearful for the safety of the driver. I grabbed a dozen or so marshalls, and we calmed ourselves down and formed a human wedge to break through the crowd to the car. I remember literally fighting off friends who were trying to get to him, shouting, "I'll kill him! I'll kill him!"

The police arrived shortly, and the sergeant and I got the driver's door open and pulled him out. As we stood face to face for a moment, I could see the hate and determination in his eyes as he looked into mine. We got him into the police car, and it sped away.

Many marchers farther back didn't know what had happened, and I ran the length of the column dispelling rumors and encouraging the crowd to keep marching. I circled the column and came up the other side. Children from a Catholic elementary school had come out to the side of the street to urge us on with smiles and peace signs. They were unaware of what had happened, and as I came running by them, each held out a hand for me to slap, saying, "Peace, brother." It was just what I needed.

When we got downtown, I called the university to see what was being reported about the attack. "What attack?" was the reply I got from the head adviser at my dormitory. "A radio report just said that a drunk had lost control of his car and accidently hit some marchers," he said. The driver was released without bond two hours later.

The incident made the CBS *Evening News*, and we learned another lesson in political reality: the police always come down hard on student protesters, but not on the violence directed against us.

The vindictive and vicious rhetoric against student protest-

ers during the Nixon years contributed directly to the violence
that was perpetrated against young people opposed to the war.
At Kent State University, we saw that America would kill its
own children for the crime of disobedience against the state.
To this day, those responsible for the Kent State killings have
never been punished nor have the deaths been officially
admitted as wrong.

We often were blamed for the violence that was done to us.
We occupied the ROTC building on campus one day, inviting
the ROTC teachers and cadets to stay and engage in a dialogue
with us about the morality of the war. After some initial
hostility from them, they opened themselves up to what
proved to be a very fruitful day of discussion, one of the most
genuinely educational events on our campus in a long time.

The sight of ROTC and antiwar students engaged in an
intense but respectful conversation was encouraging. The
dean of students showed up to survey the scene. He and I knew
each other pretty well by that time, and I personally pleaded
with him not to bring in any police and provoke a
confrontation. He offered his typical response: that he had no
control over that decision. At about three in the afternoon, I
noticed that he had left. It could mean only one thing.

A few minutes later the police arrived. Without warning,
canisters of tear gas came smashing through the windows,
sending ROTC cadets and student protesters alike fleeing the
building with burning eyes. The police went mad chasing and
hitting people, without any organized plan or purpose that I
could detect. Seemingly they did not want to arrest anybody,
but were content just to gas and club students.

The scene was tragic, and the crowd quickly scattered. Our
day of education was over, but the police had given us yet
another education. The ROTC building was damaged, most of
its windows broken. The destruction was blamed on "rioting
students."

Vietnam was a mirror in which our country could see itself.
The mirror showed the ugly image of a large and powerful
nation trying to impose its control over the destiny of a small

nation, and falling into the unspeakable brutality of attempting to destroy a people it could not master.

America refused to look at itself in the mirror that Vietnam had become. The justifications invented for our intervention in Vietnam were endless and always sounded very noble and righteous.

We said it was to protect the Vietnamese from aggression, while we invaded their country. We said it was to save them from communism, while we sought to crush their revolution for independence. We said it was to stop the Chinese or the Russian threat, while we blocked Vietnamese nationalism.

We said it was to give Vietnam democracy, while we installed and maintained a succession of corrupt and brutal dictatorships as our client regimes. We said it was for the good of the Vietnamese people, as we killed two million of them, turned twelve million more into refugees, devastated their land, and corrupted their culture. In the end, the only official reason given for prolonging the war was to "bring our boys home with their heads high," as if that were still possible. The real aim of the U.S. war in Vietnam was to destroy Vietnamese resistance to U.S. control.

To cover our nation's real purpose in Vietnam, our government resorted to lies. The war effort depended on a complex web of deception and falsehood, which the U.S. government used to justify a war that ended by devastating most of Indochina and dividing American society.

In Vietnam, the United States conducted the largest aerial bombardment in the history of warfare. More than eight million tons of explosives were dropped on the cities and countryside of Vietnam, more than all the bombs dropped in World War II and the Korean War combined. Our bombs were never restricted to military targets, as U.S. government officials claimed, but included villages, schools, hospitals, dikes, and churches.

U.S. forces engaged in "search-and-destroy" missions, killing untold civilians and burning countless villages to the ground under the pretext of looking for guerrillas. The guerrillas and the general population were virtually indistinguishable. The Vietnamese people had for centuries worked together and poured their lives into resistance efforts against foreign powers, and throughout the North and most of the South the whole population was mobilized to throw out the American intruders. American GIs reported that even small children were part of the effort.

Helicopter gunships spread machine gun fire, explosives, and napalm all over the countryside, defoliating forests and jungles and destroying rice paddies. In Vietnam we saw the widespread use of anti-personnel weaponry. For example, thousands of tiny explosives that resembled small leaves—not powerful enough to blow a truck tire but powerful enough to take off the foot of a barefoot peasant who might step on one—were dropped on the ground.

But our enormous army, rolling over the Vietnamese countryside and pounding it with almost all the brutality that military science could devise, was unable to defeat the will of the people to resist. Half a million troops, the latest and finest in war technology and chemical warfare, could not subdue the small groups of guerrilla fighters—lean, fast, mobile strike forces using hit-and-run style, moving in and out of the civilian population that was their support base and protection.

The more intense the American war effort, the stiffer seemed the resistance. We were undone by the discipline and determination of an enemy who had fought with limited supplies and sacrificial commitment day in and day out for years. Contrary to the opulent life-style of the Saigon dictators, even the North Vietnamese leaders lived on the same income as that of the average North Vietnamese peasant.

The United States never had any real hope of winning a guerrilla war that had such wide support of the indigenous population. However, American power and presence did succeed in devastating most of the country and corrupting much of its culture. American money and consumerism made the city of Saigon into an ugly reflection of mainstream American culture, quite out of place in a world of rural peasants engaged in a life and death struggle. Neon Coca-cola signs, shoeshine boys, thousands of Vietnamese village girls forced into prostitution, and a huge and lucrative black market were the principal signs of the American presence.

The official justifications for our presence in Vietnam were illusions that died hard. The sense of anger and betrayal many felt was expressed in a GI resistance pamphlet produced in Vietnam entitled *The Whole Damn Thing Was a Lie*. Many tried to reconcile the lie with drugs. At the height of the war, Saigon hospitals held more American soldiers for heroin addiction than war casualties.

The young men who were sent to Vietnam paid a heavy price. Fifty-five thousand of them died for a lie. Thousands more were wounded and maimed for life. The psychological and spiritual cost for many more is a continuing legacy. The veterans of the Vietnam War came home to a nation that treated them first with suspicion and then neglect. They have suffered isolation and rejection from a confused public not sure how to react to the defeat and ambiguity of the war.

During the years of the war, my father and I fought bitterly. I remember one particularly volatile conversation that dramatically showed the differences between us. He said to me, "Every time I see the flag go up the flagpole, I think of buddies of mine who died in World War II. A tear comes to my eye, and tingles go up and down my spine."

My response to him was, "Every time I see that flag go up the flagpole, I think of Detroit going up in flames and Vietnamese villagers being burned by the U.S. army, and it makes me sick."

With the revelation of the American massacre of Vietnamese civilians at My Lai, a significant change occurred in my father. He was deeply disillusioned by the reports and was astute enough to know that if such a tragedy had happened in one village, it was probably happening in others. His support of the war soon came to an end.

When the war was finally over, most Americans hurried to join the great national emotion of the hour: the desire to forget. The people of this country wanted to put the confusing and tragic adventure behind them, go back to business as usual, and be proud again to be Americans. I even remember reading editorials which recommended that a comforting memory lapse characterize our national mood as we seek to bind up our nation's wounds. We were simply to forget the destruction and suffering we left behind in that once beautiful little country that refused to be pounded into submission by American power.

I returned a year after the end of the war to Michigan State to give a keynote address at a conference on religion and politics. Throughout the evening I sensed a different spirit, indeed a different place, than the environment I had known in the late sixties. The questions and conversations during my short but painful return confirmed my worst fears.

Where once there had been a deep and serious questioning of the legitimacy of the American political and economic system, now there was the anxious frenzy to acquire the necessary credentials and connections to fit into that very system. The pre-eminent values of ambition, accumulation, and advancement seemed to be reproducing themselves with relative ease in the student population. Talk of confronting, resisting, building alternatives, or even questioning felt inappropriate in the new climate of self-serving realism.

On a nostalgic walk along old routes I came to the big rock, situated in the center of a large grassy area, which used to be a rallying point for teach-ins and speeches against the war. Many of our marches and demonstrations had been launched from that rock.

I sat quietly in the shadow of this monument upon which I and others used to stand and speak. I watched students pass by, seemingly unaware of its rich tradition. The place was now a curious, perhaps comic, relic of an era long gone.

But some of us will never forget. A generation of us grew up on the Vietnam War. It took us from the patriotism of our childhood through the protest of our adolescence to the resistance of our adulthood. Through Vietnam, we learned of another America, not of hope, opportunity, and pride, but of arrogance, brutality, and shame. And we have never been the same since.

Through several presidential administrations we had watched the politicians promise peace and escalate the war. We heard the official justifications for the genocide, and we were unconvinced.

Our country's involvement in Vietnam was more than just a mistake or miscalculation. Vietnam became the testing ground of American hegemony around the globe, and it showed the extent to which American power would go to achieve its purposes. What we did in seeking to control the destiny of another people was illegal and immoral. In biblical terms, this national act of selfish cruelty was a sin. But the church was largely silent.

I remember during my college years coming across a quotation from Arnold Toynbee, the great British historian, who commented during the Vietnam years on the new American role in the world: "America is today the leader of a world-wide anti-revolutionary movement in defense of vested interests. She now stands for what Rome stood for. Rome consistently supported the rich against the poor in all foreign communities that fell under her sway; and since the poor, so far, have always and everywhere been far more numerous than the rich, Rome's policy made for inequality, for injustice, and for the least happiness of the greatest number. America's decision to adopt Rome's role has been deliberate, if I have gauged it right" (*America and World Revolution*).

Toynbee's words struck me deeply. The comparison of America to Rome, the American empire to the Roman Empire, seemed both startling and true. And as I considered the quote, I couldn't help thinking of the way Rome treated Christians. It seemed to me that if Christians were living like the first-century believers, they might be treated the same way. But I saw few Christians living like those in the early church.

I remember many years later a story that Mark Hatfield told. An evangelical Christian, he was one of the first of America's elected leaders to oppose the war in Vietnam.

At the National Governors' Conference in 1965, President Lyndon Johnson asked for a vote of support for his Gulf of Tonkin Resolution, which had passed overwhelmingly in the Senate and the House of Representatives and eventually became the official justification for getting us into the war in Vietnam. The resolution passed forty-nine to one at the governors' conference; Hatfield's was the dissenting vote. Later on, as a Republican senator completely opposed to the war policies of Richard Nixon, his opposition became even more visible.

Hatfield told me about the piles of angry mail he received from evangelical Christians during those years, some beginning with "Dear Former Brother in Christ." Mark Hatfield's stand on Vietnam was rooted firmly in his Christian conviction, and such treatment at the hands of fellow believers was deeply painful to him.

The response of evangelical Christians at my university was not much different from Hatfield's Christian constituency. During my four years at MSU, I was unsuccessfully evangelized by every Christian group on campus.

The evangelical Christian groups stood out on campus for their lack of concern about the war in Vietnam. At one antiwar rally, a number of my friends wanted to expel from the scene some members of Campus Crusade for Christ who were distributing leaflets entitled *Real Peace Is Through Jesus*. I insisted that they be allowed to stay and started a conversation with one of their leaders. I asked him questions about how he felt about the war, and to each question he responded only, "Real peace is through Jesus." Finally, I confronted him directly and said, "Look, just tell me your position on the war."

"I think we should bomb the communists off the map," was his reply. And I could answer only, "Yeah, that's what I thought you meant by real peace through Jesus." It seemed that things hadn't changed much in the evangelical world since I had been away from it.

The Inter-Varsity Christian Fellowship members weren't ardent cold warriors like the Campus Crusaders, but they could never quite figure out what they thought about the war. They were very cautious by temperament, had a fear of anything political, and committed themselves only to pray about the war. When it was over, some of them told me they had decided that the war was wrong, a conclusion that they came to too late. Had they arrived at it earlier, their witness could have been helpful to many students.

There were a few liberal campus ministers who were against the war. They offered us their facilities, attended our rallies, let us know they were behind us, and one even once told me that the antiwar movement was "the real church."

But they had little to say about what Christian faith had to do with our lives or the struggle for peace. Their motivations, as far as I could tell, were mostly political. I'm not sure it was clear to most of them why they should be involved in the movement as Christians. To many of them the movement seemed more a student activity to be involved in than a clear and public demonstration of Christian conscience.

I had been told by my church at home that Christian faith had nothing to do with the questions that were creating such a passion in me: racism, poverty, and war. Ironically, from the other side, the message of the liberal ministers was the same, which was unfortunate. Many of the deepest personal and political questions with which I and other antiwar leaders were struggling could have been responded to by Christian faith. The movement was much weaker for lack of the things that an active Christian presence might have contributed.

Those questions and struggles were perhaps most focused in 1968, a crucial year for me. When Dr. Martin Luther King, Jr., was assassinated, a lot of my hope died with him. For many of us who had grown disillusioned with America's white leadership, black leaders were the only public figures in America who were articulating the protest and vision we shared. King's courageous stand against the war in Vietnam, combined with his tireless advocacy on behalf of his own people, made him a leader of us all.

Martin Luther King was probably the greatest political

leader produced by America in the twentieth century. He was one of the very few people who had a vision for the future of America worthy of its ideals. He was genuinely a prophet in the tradition of the Old Testament, and his death diminished us all.

A short time later, Robert Kennedy was assassinated. Kennedy had slowly allowed himself to be touched by the experience of American poor people, especially blacks and Hispanics, and they recognized in him a genuine concern for their lives. He also began to see that the war his brother had escalated was morally wrong, and he was beginning to turn against it.

Kennedy's conversion was still in process when he was killed, but I think the change was genuine. How far it may have gone for this man is hard to tell. It would have meant a break with the political establishment, the ruling class which spawned him, and even his own family. But he was the only elected official in whom I placed any hope. I followed his presidential campaign in 1968 with intense interest, and I decided that if he won the Democratic nomination I would go to work for him.

I remember staying up late the night of the California primary listening to the radio. The tide had turned, and it looked as though Robert Kennedy would take the state. With that victory, the chances of challenging Hubert Humphrey looked very strong. I turned off the radio and went to bed that night with a feeling of great excitement.

I woke up early the next day and turned the radio on. The first words I heard were, "Robert Kennedy has been shot." It wasn't long before it was reported that he was dead. I wept bitterly. A good man who might have been a great leader had been cut down in the prime of his life. The last hope of ending the war and bringing change through the electoral system was dead.

It was a tough spring and summer, I recall, culminating in the Democratic National Convention in Chicago. Inside the convention hall, Richard Daley, Hubert Humphrey, and the Democratic Party trampled on whatever political hope was left for peace and justice, while Daley's police busted heads outside in the streets. I watched on television the battle in the streets of Chicago, and I remember how strongly I felt about wanting to be there to fight Daley's police. The convention was a peak of intense frustration, anger, and hopelessness for many of us.

The political system seemed more repressive than ever. It was during this time that I felt an increasing identification with revolutionary movements around the world and more direct personal sympathy and political support for the Viet Cong, who were young men just like me fighting in the jungles against the same system that I was fighting at home.

The romance of the movement was gone for me. Continuing experience with the unresponsiveness of political, economic, and educational institutions, much study, and lessons learned from police clubs and tear gas had turned me from an idealistic social crusader into a more sober, politically wise, more radical activist and organizer, ready to commit the rest of my life to resisting the system that oppressed the poor at home and killed them in Vietnam.

A year later, in October of 1969, moratorium marches calling for an immediate and unconditional withdrawal from Vietnam attracted millions of people all over the country to the streets. The next month, half a million people came to Washington to protest the war in the largest political demonstration in American history up to that time. That event was extraordinary.

I remember sitting on the grass surrounding the Washington Monument, watching a sea of people that stretched in every direction as far as the eye could see. The great old folk singer and organizer Pete Seeger got us all to stand up and rock together with arms in the air, singing "All We Are Saying Is Give Peace a Chance." My eyes were filled with tears and my heart with hope.

I felt again that afternoon the revival spirit that I had grown up with, but it was much deeper this time. This was the kind of revival in which I believed: one that spoke about justice, mercy, and peace. If faith meant anything, it had to speak for these issues. I turned to the friend next to me, with whom I had organized for years, and said, "How could they possibly ignore such a tremendous outpouring of public sentiment?"

But ignore it they did—or so they said. Richard Nixon and his attorney general, John Mitchell, made a great public point of the fact that they had been watching the Michigan-Ohio State football game during the demonstration and had never bothered to look out the window. We didn't learn until later, with Daniel Ellsberg's revelations from government documents, that the antiwar movement had a strong impact on government policy, continually limiting the government's options and perhaps preventing the United States from using nuclear weapons in Vietnam.

This peak of the movement was also the beginning of its demise. Nixon soon unfurled his policy of "Vietnamization"—bringing home U.S. troops while totally supplying the South Vietnamese army and stepping up the air war. It was an utterly cynical and callous policy, based totally on calculated American self-interest, one that we called merely "changing the color of the corpses."

The policy was designed to lower American casualties and thereby defuse antiwar sentiment in the United States. At the same time the plan called for intensifying the aerial bombardment of Vietnam with the application of still more highly sophisticated technical firepower, chemical warfare, and anti-personnel weaponry. The central feature of the policy was the ending of the draft, which Nixon was sure would take the energy out of the student antiwar movement.

As leaders of that movement, we were sure he was wrong. But he was proven right. The black leaders with whom we had worked in coalition on a number of issues had always told us that they didn't trust our constituency: "We trust a few of you as individuals, but as soon as this war is over, all your people are going to go back to life as usual and forget all about the problems of black people—again." They were wrong only in that most students quit before the war ended.

Even in the spring of 1970 during the national student strike we began to feel that the end of the student movement was near. The ending of the draft, the Vietnamization of the war, the killings at Kent State, the increase of domestic surveillance and repression, and, of course, graduation, were all taking their toll. The change occurred quickly. From being able to get ten thousand people in the street in a few hours, we found ourselves sitting around in a small circle again with a "faithful few."

The experience taught me some painful but valuable lessons about the role of self-interest in the politics of mass movements. Public sentiment remained strong and even grew until the Vietnamese won their victory some years later, but the commitment of young students to opposing the war was on the decline and continued to diminish. Most students were still against the war but became less and less willing to make personal sacrifices to oppose it.

For those of us who had been leaders in the student antiwar movement, it was a time for reflection, both personal and political, for the sorting out of our lives and future directions. Some of my fellow radicals talked of armed revolution, while others spoke of graduate school. Many had a tough time deciding between the two.

In most cases, the choice for revolutionary struggle was short-lived, and most student radicals eventually found their way into respectable and responsible careers. Some are now teaching courses on the sixties and the New Left in political science departments of major universities. For them, the revolution didn't come, but tenure did.

My reflection took me back to the New Testament.

4
Finding My Way Back

Although my alienation from the church became a complete break during my years in the antiwar movement, I could never quite get shed of Jesus. He seemed to have taken up permanent, though quiet, residence somewhere in my soul, and at this critical point in my life he resurfaced to lead me back to himself.

With the student movement coming to an end, I needed time to sort out my life. After graduation from the university, I withdrew from political activity for a few months, got an apartment off campus with some friends, took a manual labor job, and settled into reflection about where I had been and where I was going.

In my teen-age years I had been faced with a clear choice. I could have stayed in the comfortable world of family, church, and friends, putting aside my growing restlessness about racism and the war. But I chose instead to follow the direction my heart was leading me—into the city, close to the poor, against the war. It was a path of loneliness and uncertainty.

My confrontations with the church had taken a heavy toll, and I angrily rejected it as it had rejected me. I had been too young to understand the fears of the church members and their entrapment in the culture. I felt only their lack of concern. My idealism and even my faith had been shattered by their response to my attempts to exercise Christian conscience.

During the years I was in college I was distant from the church and any formal belief system, but those years were religious in many ways. I was preoccupied with ultimate questions, questions of purpose and meaning. The "why" was always more important than the "how," and I delved into philosophy, theology, and ethics in a search for answers.

I poured my passion into the student movement with the faith of a zealot. Stopping the war became a religion for me. But I began to lose my faith in the movement even before its demise was in sight.

Marxist analysis was attractive to me in those years, but I was increasingly disillusioned with the patronizing and arrogant attitudes of left-wing ideologues who saw the poor mostly as a constituency to be organized. I wondered who would have the power in their new regime; I doubted that it would be poor people. And those who were so oppressed and wretched as to be unorganizable held little attraction for my friends on the left. The capitalists exploit the poor, but the communists use their oppression as a means to power.

The Left also readily accepted the assumptions about violence and the manipulation of power that were the operational characteristics of the established order. Across the political spectrum, everyone seemed to agree that the end justified the means. My thinking was changing on this issue.

And I had had my fill of the ego struggles and personal rivalries in the movement. The personal, sexual, and political exploitation mirrored the system we were fighting.

The movement, I think, represented the best idealism of our time. It raised the questions the church should have raised. It attacked injustice, fought racism, and opposed war, all Christian vocations that were for the most part abandoned by the church during those years and left to secular prophets.

But the movement, unable to generate enough vision or resources for spiritual and political transformation, had an inadequate basis both for protest and affirmation and could never live up to its promises. It ended up being confounded by the same weakness and sin that beset the surrounding culture.

I had long been searching for something that would transform both personal and political life. The movement had been a significant part of my formation, my home for several years. But no longer did it have the answers to my deepest longings and questions.

This realization took me back to the New Testament. I wanted to take one last look at Christian faith. I wanted to look at the Bible again with as fresh a perspective as I could bring to it.

With new earnestness, I searched the Bible for answers. I read mostly in the Gospels, and I discovered the wholeness of the gospel message for the first time. It was as though the Jesus who had always been there on the edges of my life revealed himself to me clearly.

I concentrated on the Sermon on the Mount. It was startling to me that I could not recall a sermon ever preached on this manifesto of Christ's new social order in my church when I was growing up. I vaguely remembered some talk about the Sermon on the Mount not being applicable to our time, that it was meant for the time when we all would get to heaven.

The Sermon revealed to me what Jesus meant by the kingdom of God. In it, Jesus calls those who would follow him to a life that completely undermines the values and structures of this world and opens up possibilities of a new one. The way of life described in the Sermon is truly revolutionary, much deeper and more radical than the revolutionary movements of which I had had a taste. The way of Jesus overturns the assumptions of Right, Left, and Middle, and presents a genuinely new option for both our personal and political lives. It calls for a life lived for God, for neighbor, for the poor, and even for enemies.

I read on through the gospel narratives and the parables in which Jesus describes the ways that God's new order might become real in the lives of men and women during the political turmoil of first-century, Roman-occupied Palestine. The gospel story captured my imagination. All of my excitement about the new life I was discovering culminated for me when I read Matthew 25:

"When the Son of Man comes in his glory, and all the angels with him, then he will sit on his glorious throne. Before him will be gathered all the nations, and he will separate them one from another as a shepherd separates the sheep from the goats, and he will place the sheep at his right hand, but the goats at the left. Then the King will say to those at his right hand, 'Come, O blessed of my Father, inherit the kingdom prepared for you from the foundation of the world; for I was hungry and you gave me food, I was thirsty and you gave me drink, I was a stranger and you welcomed me, I was naked and you clothed me, I was sick and you visited me, I was in prison and you came to me.' Then the righteous will answer him, 'Lord, when did we see thee hungry and feed thee, or thirsty and give thee drink? And when did we see thee a stranger and welcome thee, or naked and clothe thee? And when did we see thee sick or in prison and visit thee?' And the King will answer them, 'Truly, I say to you, as you did it to one of the least of these my [brothers and sisters], you did it to me.' Then he will say to those at his left hand, 'Depart from me, you cursed, into the eternal fire prepared for the devil and his angels; for I was hungry and you gave me no food, I was thirsty and you gave me no drink, I was a stranger and you did not welcome me, naked and you did not clothe me, sick and in prison and you did not visit me.' Then they also will answer, 'Lord, when did we see thee hungry or thirsty or a stranger or naked or sick or in prison, and did not minister to thee?' Then he will answer them, 'Truly, I say to you, as you did it not to one of the least of these, you did it not to me.' And they will go away into eternal punishment, but the righteous into eternal life."

(Matt. 25:31-46)

This was my conversion passage. I was deeply struck by a God who had taken up residence among the poor, the oppressed, the outcasts. How much we love Jesus, this passage tells us, is determined by how much we serve those who are at the bottom of society.

The connections began to come clear. I knew that my most important lessons had been taught to me in the black community and in opposition to a war that was claiming so many innocent Vietnamese lives. I began to see that this was not coincidence, but spiritual logic.

The truth about a society is best known at the bottom, among its victims. That is where Jesus is most present, most at home, and where we most easily learn of his way. Jesus had been with me, and is among us all the time, in the guise of the poor.

To find our way back to Jesus means a pilgrimage into the world of the hungry, the homeless, the disenfranchised. In America that means that Jesus can best be discovered in the ghettos, the barrios, the welfare offices and unemployment lines, the prisons. In the broader world, he is among the victims of war, in the refugee camps, with the prisoners for conscience' sake. No wonder I hadn't known Jesus very well; I hadn't been shown where to look for him.

I finally knew that I wanted to be a follower of this Jesus. Contrary to the message I had received from the church, Jesus' message was as political as it was personal, as economic as it was spiritual, having as much to do with public life as individual devotion. Jesus had lived and preached and died to begin a new order that would turn the world upside down and change lives and history in every way.

Jesus was not only the savior of my soul, he was a Lord to whom I was offering my political allegiance. His way was a visible and viable alternative to the ideologies and systems that were vying for power in the world.

This was a crossroads time for me, one for making choices and decisions, but it was not an emotional crisis, nor was I feeling desperate or overcome with religious guilt. I simply knew that I had to make a choice about how I was going to live my life and to what or to whom I was going to give myself.

During my months of immersion in the Bible, I had no contact with Christians or the church. I had only my own background, my reflections and experience, and my Bible. Mine was a very private struggle, but after a few months I felt hungry to learn from others.

I had always had an interest in theological study, so I decided to go to seminary, believing that the experience would ground me in my newly rediscovered faith. I had become quite disillusioned with political liberalism and suspected that theological liberalism was its first cousin, so I chose a conservative evangelical seminary. I wanted to go to a place where the Bible was believed and its message taken seriously. In the fall of 1970, I packed all my belongings into the trunk of my Ford Falcon and drove from Michigan to a section of Deerfield, Illinois, called Bannockburn.

I arrived at Trinity Evangelical Divinity School with my heart fervent with the hope of the gospel and my mind grappling with the connection between faith and our historical situation. The war was still raging under the presidency of Richard Nixon, and was, I thought, the most immediate and urgent test of Christian conscience.

My first night at seminary, I met my next-door neighbor in the dormitory and talked with him about my disillusionment with the evangelical church's support of the war in Vietnam and its indifference to racism. He shared the same feelings, and we had a conversation that lasted through the night. I talked with him about my background, experience in the movement, and conversion. And I spoke of my hopes for recovering the prophetic biblical tradition, the authentic evangelical message, and applying it to our historical situation. We talked even that first night with great excitement about the possibilities of a new meaning of the gospel for our times. The morning came without either of us having a thought of tiredness.

In our excitement about the possibilities, we decided that the place to begin was the seminary. I thought we needed a group of students to start with, a community of sorts. We agreed to keep our eyes and ears open the next couple of days to find out who might be interested in joining us. In the cafeteria line, on the way to classes, in the dorms, we listened and talked with other students. Soon the first meeting of a handful of Trinity seminary students was convened in my room.

This was the beginning of a long and deep relationship between us, and the inception of what is now Sojourners

Fellowship. Twelve years later, almost all of us are pursuing the vision of the gospel that excited us at the beginning. Two of the group, Joe Roos and Bob Sabath, are pastors with me at Sojourners; John Topliff is one of the leaders of the Menominee River Fellowship in Michigan's upper peninsula, the other community that emerged from our days at Trinity; Boyd Reese is a member of Jubilee Fellowship in Philadelphia; Barry Turner is an Episcopal priest in California; Herb McMullen is entering the Episcopal priesthood in Washington, D.C.; and Dennis McDonald teaches New Testament at Iliff Seminary in Denver.

Now scattered around the country, most of us in that early group remember our days at Trinity as the most formative period of our Christian ministry. It was a deeply bonding time based on a common vision and close friendship. I will always treasure that unique time which gave birth to Sojourners and all that it represents.

We met almost every night in one of our dorm rooms for study and intense discussion. Those evenings were filled with talk, prayer, laughter, and tears. It was a time of visions and dreams, for the church and for our own lives.

On weekends we often continued our discussions at Bill's Pub, where the peanuts were free and the beer two dollars a pitcher. We were not your ordinary pub patrons. I will never forget the evening our waitress discovered us all bowed in intense prayer, hands locked across the table; she couldn't figure out where to put the pitcher.

If we didn't blend into the woodwork at Bill's, it was becoming increasingly clear that we didn't fit in at the seminary either. The radical call to the kingdom that had captured our commitment was completely different from the evangelical cultural religion so deeply entrenched at the seminary. The school became an often hostile environment where we hammered out our theology.

We were simply trying to do what the seminary encouraged its students to do: take the Bible seriously. It was our biblical study and reflection that was now the basis for our opposition to the war in Vietnam and our solidarity with the poor. And it was that same reflection that led us to question the very foundation and operation of the economic system in which the seminary was so deeply enmeshed.

After several weeks of meetings, our little group decided to put together a statement. I was assigned the task of writing it. I was working at the time as a night watchman in a local high school. I worked through the night on the statement, interrupted every two hours by having to make my rounds with a flashlight through the dark school. I put my whole heart into the writing, knowing that my conversion had been leading to this opportunity to say what I believed about "radical discipleship."

I finished the statement by morning and hurried back to the seminary for a day of classes. That evening the group gathered again in my room for the official reading of our manifesto. It was a dramatic moment for all of us as I read the text, which included the following statements:

> The church has failed to adequately communicate the gospel of Jesus Christ to our culture. . . . Because Christians are not living the gospel they are proclaiming, the church has become tragically irrelevant to our times and problems, and is losing touch with the world we live in. . . .
>
> The church lacks a dynamic, biblical social ethic in this time of great national and world crisis. Never has our world so needed the prophetic voice of the church. The Scriptures are clear in condemning social and economic injustice, oppression, racism, hypocrisy, environmental destruction, and the kind of chauvinistic nationalism that gives rise to aggression, imperialism, and endless war. To these critical issues and other forms of human suffering, the church today has been silent, indifferent, or even stubbornly reactionary—fighting against necessary change, supporting and sanctifying the status quo. . . . Biblical instruction is clear in teaching that faith divorced from social justice is a mockery. True spirituality manifests itself in a concern for the needs and rights of people.

I hoped that I had expressed what we all wanted to say and wondered what the response would be. I felt almost like a preacher putting out an altar call and waiting for the people to come forward. After the reading, the room was quiet for a moment, and then the confirmation came in a wave. We had our message.

We typed the statement and took it to the seminary administrative offices to ask about using their photocopy machine, offering to pay for its use. The person in charge read the statement and told us that we couldn't use the machine. This was the beginning of our political conflict with the seminary. We ended up running it off at the nearby Unitarian church, which offered to do it free of charge.

The next morning we handed out copies of the statement at the seminary and its denominational college across the street. Trinity had never been leafletted before, and our action became more controversial than we could ever have imagined. Apparently these evangelical institutions had completely missed the sixties.

The seven of us who had signed the statement soon became referred to as the "Bannockburn Seven" and were henceforth known in the seminary community as "the radicals." The word began to spread that something new was happening at Trinity.

Rumors spread far and wide. One that reached all the way to California after I had been at Trinity only a few weeks was that the seminary had allowed in a radical SDS (Students for a Democratic Society) student who had led riots at Michigan State University.

One of the best rumors came in the spring of 1971. Our group had just held a demonstration on campus protesting the way the administration was, in our view, ignoring student opinion. At a mock funeral complete with a trumpet rendition of "Taps," we "buried student opinion" in front of the administration building. Bob Sabath, away on a study quarter in France, heard from American missionaries in that country that "seven bearded radicals" had burned in effigy the dean of the seminary, Kenneth Kantzer.

Each week we held a "free university," a forum which drew a hundred students who were interested in a variety of social, political, and theological issues, from the war and racism to discrimination against women. We also kept a literature table stacked with antiwar material outside the mail room and student lounge. We got involved in antiwar work in nearby Chicago and gave many students at Trinity their first taste of demonstrations and marches.

Although our behavior wasn't unusual as campus activity went in the country at the time, it was quite unusual for a leading evangelical seminary. And unlike activists on most other campuses, we held regular Bible studies and worship celebrations, which were gathering places for seminary and college students as well as for local teen-agers. These became a focal point of an evangelistic ministry we carried on for troubled teen-agers in the area, an unexpected activity for a group like ours with such a strong commitment to social justice.

These were serious worship and social events, despite the name we gave to them ("God parties") and the choice of "Joy to the World" as our traditional opening song (the Three Dog Night version beginning, "Jeremiah was a bullfrog . . .").

We generated a great deal of controversy and excitement. More and more students and some faculty members began to respond to what we were saying and doing, some offering support and others opposition and hostility.

Many of the students who attended our gatherings are now pastors in churches. To this day I still meet some of them when I'm on the road speaking, and occasionally I receive thankful letters telling me about how being part of those tumultuous times at Trinity has helped shape their ministry.

Some very close and significant relationships with individual faculty members developed, most notably with Clark Pinnock, a professor of theology. Clark was at once a teacher, a brother, and a friend. He is a man of deep personal integrity, exceptional intellectual capacity, and genuine Christian conscience. He was an early supporter and counselor for our efforts at Trinity and stood by us in the controversy, even at risk to his own position at the seminary.

I was often in trouble with the administration. I remember

one time being asked to appear before the seminary's board of trustees to give my personal testimony of faith in Jesus Christ. Bair Lake campfires came to mind. I think the trustees needed to be convinced that I was really a Christian.

There were even efforts to dismiss me from school. I remember the "special interviews" set up in 1972 to determine whether the seminary would allow me to stay. I was told: "It's not that we don't trust your sincerity and integrity. It's not that your concerns are unbiblical. It's not that you don't have a real ministry here. . . . It's just that the presence of you and your friends has cost the seminary almost a million dollars in lost contributions. We just can't afford to keep you here."

Dean Kantzer and I formed a personal relationship during all the turmoil. He tried his best to allow us to continue as students, and I tried to help him with the problems he had with the seminary's faculty and constituency over us. He was trying to grant us academic freedom and at the same time keep a school that was already in financial trouble going, a most difficult task.

One day I received a phone call from Joan Bissett in the registrar's office, who with her husband, Steve, had joined our group and were later among the founders of the Menominee River Fellowship. "Guess who just came to see you?" she said to me. I'm sure it was the only time the FBI had ever visited Trinity, or for that matter any other evangelical institution in those years. It is to the seminary's credit that, when the FBI agents identified themselves and asked for information on me and some of the others in the group, it refused to comply.

Trinity had never encountered a situation like the one we were creating and was totally unprepared for it. Suddenly a conservative evangelical seminary had a radical student movement on its hands. That movement was in the dormitories and classrooms, was growing and spilling into the streets. It was spreading beyond the borders of the campus, causing mounting excitement among some people and deep reaction among others.

A dozen years later, it is no longer unusual to find evangelical Christians who have come to radical conclusions about the meaning of their faith in the world. A socially sensitive evangelical movement has been growing for some time and is now a viable option with a significant constituency within the evangelical community. But that was not so in the early seventies, and our little group and the seminary made a lot of trouble for each other.

We carried our concerns far beyond Trinity and Chicago. A number of us went to raise the issue of war at Explo '72, a week of training for Christian witness sponsored by Campus Crusde for Christ. Young people from all over North America gathered in the Cotton Bowl in Dallas, Texas, to hear music, testimonies, and speeches by Bill Bright, Billy Graham, and others. The cheering and clapping and shouts of "Praise the Lord" filled the stadium.

Our group set up booths to distribute literature on Christian peacemaking. On the second day of the rally, some Campus Crusade officials called us in to their headquarters and questioned us about the literature, explaining that it was not in harmony with the purposes of Explo. We gave our testimony about Christ being the Prince of Peace and the Lord whom we all followed. After much dialogue the meeting ended, and we continued our distribution.

We had made signs that said, "Stop the war in Jesus' name," "The 300 persons killed today by American bombs will not be reached in this generation," and "Choose this day—make disciples or make bombs, love your enemies or kill your enemies." We walked among the people carrying the signs and were asked, "Why bring peripheral issues to Explo? We are here to witness to the Lord."

Part of one evening's celebration in the Cotton Bowl was a Flag Day ceremony, which included personal testimonies of faith and patriotism by military officers. A delegation from South Vietnam received a standing ovation.

Our group was sitting tucked away near the top of the bleachers in one of the end zones of the great stadium. We unfurled banners which read "Cross or Flag" and "Christ or

Country." Steve Bissett said to me, "We're so far away up here, no one can see these. I think we should chant something."

I looked at him with skepticism and said, "But, Steve, there are a hundred thousand people here, clapping and cheering. Who will hear us?"

"God will hear us," was his reply. That was good enough for me.

Just at the moment we began to chant, unknown to us, the speaker on the podium had called for a moment of silence to remember our boys in Vietnam. Instead of being drowned out by noise and cheers, a little cadre of voices shouted into the silence, "Stop the war! Stop the war!" And soon a hundred thousand faces turned and looked up at our banners.

The largest billow of "boos" I had ever heard came rushing back at us. The noise was frightening, and I was scared that we might be attacked. Fifty police rushed up and surrounded us. One of them asked, "Who's in charge here?" Peter Ediger, a Mennonite pastor, answered, "The Holy Spirit."

The sergeant had obviously never dealt with the Holy Spirit before and didn't know quite what to do next. "Will you promise never to do this again?" he asked. Peter spoke up, "We'll have to see how the Spirit leads."

A man in a coat and tie came running up to me and said breathlessly, "Are you the ones who just said 'stop the war'?" I nodded. He looked agitated, and I was afraid he was going to hit me. As I cringed and closed my eyes, he said, "Thank the Lord. It's about time somebody said that. I want to be arrested with you." He was a member of the Church of the Brethren in Elgin, Illinois.

We were not arrested, but the next morning the *Dallas Morning News* carried the following front-page headline: "War vs. Peace at Explo '72." The opening paragraph of the news report said of the night before: "The Christian militants of the Prince of Peace and the might of the military were both in evidence last night in the Cotton Bowl."

Our group then put together a statement that we distributed at special meetings of military personnel at Explo:

We are deeply troubled by the continuing identification of Jesus Christ with the military. . . . There are evangelical Christians who believe that faithfulness to Christ calls us to abandon all carnal warfare; that love for God has integrity only when expressed in love for fellow-men (sic); that it is not by might nor by power but by the Lord's Spirit that we are saved from any principalities and powers of evil in our world. . . . Our ultimate allegiance is to Christ. The evangelical church's silent complicity with the immoral American involvement in Indochina is a tragic example of misplaced allegiance.

It was that kind of statement, public witness, and resulting notoriety that led us into trouble not only at Trinity but in the broader evangelical world. Our little group at Trinity had impact far beyond our numbers and significance only because few others were saying or doing publicly what we were.

Two other experiences were especially significant for me in taking our message beyond the seminary. Clark Pinnock had been invited by Inter-Varsity Christian Fellowship to lead a mission in Austin at the University of Texas. It was customary for a faculty member to take along a few students to lead workshops at events such as this. Because I was just off the university campus and involved in the integration of evangelical faith and the kinds of issues that had been sweeping the campuses, he asked me to go along. Three other students, seniors whom I had never met before, also went.

The University of Texas is a beautiful place. I remember upon arrival looking across its huge plaza with a view of the state capitol and thinking to myself, "Somebody sure could do some great organizing here."

The concourse bustled with activity. In the center stood tables with Christian literature. Next to these were the tables of the radical students. The two groups rarely spoke with each other. The Christians wrote the radicals off as being merely political—misguided at best, disloyal at worst. The radicals thought the Christians were simply spiritual—religious apologists for American power whose false piety didn't care about the bombing of Vietnamese villages.

Speeches were common on the concourse. When the Christians brought in speakers, the radicals either turned away from them with a yawn or heckled them. When the radicals sponsored speakers, the Christians either ignored them or criticized them for being Marxists or anti-Americans.

In this setting, Inter-Varsity put a microphone into my hand and told me to start speaking. I had done that many times before, but this time my message was different.

I started as I had always done, talking about the war, and a crowd soon gathered. Both radical students and Christians were surprised to hear an evangelical speaking so strongly against the war. I moved on to talk about my conversion to Jesus and spoke of how the kingdom of God was an alternative to the war system.

My street speaking was transformed into street preaching, and it felt good. It was the old kind of gospel preaching, preaching Jesus as an alternative to the world's violence. But on that campus at that time it was a whole new idea. And the crowd responded.

I had a deep empathy for the antiwar students in particular, because that's who I had been. I wanted to present to them the Jesus I had found, to tell them how the gospel had begun to answer the questions that had been on my mind and in my heart. Many of them opened up later in long personal and political conversations and said that this was the first time they had spoken to a Christian whose political perspective they could trust. They were vulnerable and receptive to the radical gospel message.

The Christians too seemed to discover fresh dimensions and implications of their faith and made new commitments to the world. As both groups opened up to the gospel, they also slowly opened up to each other.

After three days of street preaching and debate, we drove home full of hope and excitement. This had been a test of our seminary group's ideas in a secular context, and our message had met with a high level of response and involvement. When we got back to the seminary, the three other students and their wives joined our group, and reports of the events in Austin strengthened the movement at Trinity.

A few months later the president of the student body at Taylor University, an evangelical Christian college in Indiana, visited me. He told me that he had heard about the things going on at Trinity and wanted to talk. We spent the afternoon together.

At the end of the time, he said that he was looking for a speaker for a gathering of Christian student leaders from all over the country to be held at Oral Roberts University. He was convinced that I was that speaker.

I felt our group wasn't ready for such an event, the annual meeting of the cream of the crop from all the evangelical colleges. For a group still developing its ideas, it seemed like too much too soon. And since we were working as a community at Trinity, I felt uncomfortable about being singled out to be flown to Tulsa, Oklahoma, to give a speech. He left disappointed.

He called me two weeks later to say that he and the other conference planners had been praying about it ever since our meeting and really believed that I was the right one to come. I was still reluctant, but said that I would talk it over with the others.

The group talked me into it, reminding me that I wouldn't be speaking for myself but for all of us and that I would be sharing the important things that were happening among us. They told me that even though I would be going alone, they would all be with me there in spirit. Since they all thought it was such a great opportunity, I agreed for the first time to be flown to a faraway city to talk about Jesus. I must confess that in all the years since then I still have mixed feelings every time I get on a plane to do that.

I arrived during the evening session the night before I was scheduled to speak. As I entered the crowded auditorium, I heard the speaker say, "I want to report to you all that my good friend Lon Nol is recovering from his illness and will soon be out of the hospital, again leading his people in their heroic fight against communism."

The speaker was Stanley Mooneyham, the president of World Vision, the powerful evangelical relief agency. The good friend he referred to was the corrupt military dictator whom the United States installed in Cambodia after the CIA helped arrange a coup to overthrow the legitimate government of Prince Sihanouk.

Lon Nol and his despicable regime were a handful of wealthy aristocrats who cooperated with the American war effort in Indochina at the expense of their own people. They gave the U.S. government permission to bomb the Cambodian countryside, which signaled the beginning of the devastation and destablization of Cambodia that would later lead to the massive slaughter of the Cambodian people by the Pol Pot government.

That night a major evangelical leader, head of a powerful evangelical organization, made his support for the American war effort absolutely clear. That was quite a sobering introduction to the conference for me. I felt very alone that night, wrestling with what I would say the next day and wondering how this group of future evangelical leaders would respond.

I was introduced the next night to an auditorium full of scrubbed, young, white faces, looking as all-American as they could be. I was described as "an ex-radical student leader who had become a Christian." Apart from that, the audience knew nothing about me or our group at Trinity. I rose to speak, and at that moment I could literally feel the support, presence, and prayers of my friends back home.

I explained that I had grown up as an evangelical, just like most of them. I spoke of the hurt of the cities, of the broken lives and spirits of black people. I shared painfully about how the white churches had shown that they didn't care about racism and the poor who had suffered so much.

Then I began to talk about the war, about the Vietnamese people and what we were doing to their country. I told them that the war was more than illegal, it was a sin against the people of Vietnam and against the God who loved them as much as he loved us.

I said that the church's silence in the face of such massive violence was an abomination before God, and it could only mean that conscience had fled the church, leaving our hearts cold and numb. Because the church had said and done nothing about the war in Southeast Asia and the war against the poor in our own land, God had raised up others to speak, but now their voices were faltering too as they were beset by confusion and self-interest.

Then I spoke of Jesus, of his Sermon on the Mount and of his presence among the lowly and the poor. I talked of his kingdom and his way of peace. I testified that he had reached out and brought me home to himself in the midst of my own struggles and confusion. I said that he had called me and others at my seminary, and was calling all of us, to a new understanding of who he was and what he wanted us to do.

I exhorted them to break with their conformity to American values, to preach and live the gospel that is a message of peace and good news to the poor. I pointed out that as Christians we could no longer support the violence of this country against the unfortunate multitudes who stood in the way of American interests.

As young Christians, it was our duty to do more than condemn the church for its failings, but to build a new church, beginning with our own lives. We had to build a church that would love the poor the way God did, that wouldn't be controlled by its culture or ruled by its government. I explained that if we did that we could help restore the authentic biblical tradition, that we could recover the gospel for our times.

All the while I was talking, I could see in their eyes what I've seen in the eyes of many people since: a hunger for deeper faith. They were listening with their ears, but I could see that the message was going right to their hearts.

Their faces had a look of new understanding, of hearing in a way that they had never heard before. Just as I had experienced in my own reading of the Bible, their vague intuitions, hopes, and fears were suddenly brought together and given articulation in a way that helped them understand for the first time the meaning of the uneasiness that had been growing inside of them.

I was warmed and overwhelmed by their response of applause, cheers, and tears. I had spoken that night of very difficult things, and yet the feeling in the room was one of joy, of being on the edge of new possibilities. I had felt for some time that we couldn't be alone in what we were thinking at Trinity, that God had to be bringing the same message to others and that people were as ready to receive it as we had been. Now I knew it was true.

I wasn't left alone the rest of the weekend. Every time I sat down or even stood still, a crowd of students gathered to talk, sometimes for hours. As Austin had been a testing ground for the message in a secular context, Tulsa was the same in a Christian setting. Something happened that weekend that held the promise of the new evangelical movement in America of which I had dreamed.

The evangelical faith on which those students had been raised had too small a heart, too small to encompass the poor and suffering, the victims of the war in Vietnam. Yet their hearts were larger than the narrow faith they had been given. They were ready for more. They longed for it, and they knew they needed it.

When they heard the message, it all made sense to them. There was such a desire among them for commitment to the radical claims of the gospel, I knew that something was going on that was much larger than any of us, that something new was being born in the heart of the evangelical community, and nothing could stop its emergence.

I went back to Chicago utterly exhausted, but full of excitement. What had captured our imaginations, fired our spirits, and called us to commitment was being confirmed by the response of others.

We had often spoken at Trinity of the American captivity of

the church and how we longed to see the church break out of its cultural chains. But even in saying that, we found ourselves in a posture that put us against the church. Now we were beginning to feel a love for that church and a commitment to rebuild it.

That call became a personal one for me. I remember a conference I went to much later at the Kirkridge Retreat Center in the Pocono Mountains of Pennsylvania with religious activists from all over the East Coast. I hitchhiked from Chicago in the rain and arrived in the middle of the night.

The next morning each of us was asked to make a sign, write on it what we felt was our most pressing concern and pin it to our shirt. Each of these activists had a particular concern for the war, human rights, or poverty. I remember writing, "The rebuilding of the church."

The contrast between my sign and the others was startling, even to me. I had begun to see that the dynamic power of the gospel was alive in spite of a church whose witness and life-style served to hide and contradict that power. I felt it was time for the church to rediscover its identity. In writing that sign I was finally articulating what I had begun to feel after my time in Tulsa and knew in the deepest parts of me was my overarching concern.

Tulsa gave me the feeling that our biblical faith was destined to turn the world upside down. I believed that the evangelical affirmation of America would be turned on its head and that some day the authorities would fear those who took the Bible seriously.

Our group became even more determined to break free of the cultural captivity that had so crippled the life of the church and to see the power of the gospel restored once again. We had the feeling of being in on the beginning of a movement, which literally consumed us. We talked about it wherever we went, and the message was spreading.

All these experiences were fresh in our minds when we decided to publish a newspaper that would give expression to all that we were feeling about the gospel and be a vehicle for a new movement of Christian conscience.

5
A Magazine
and a Community

While in seminary, I turned in a raft of course papers with titles like, "The Social Implications of the Old Testament Prophets," "The Political Implications of the Early Church," "The Social and Political Implications of New Testament Eschatology." What had captured my passion was obvious.

Our little group was discovering that all these social implications were beginning to have social implications among us as well. The bonds between us had grown so strong that by the spring of 1971 we felt ready to move in together and put out a publication that would give our concerns a wider hearing.

The *Post-American* was born in the home of the Jolly Green Giant. One of our group had noticed a sign on a seminary bulletin board: the owner of a large house in a nearby suburb of Chicago was looking for students to live there and paint his house during the summer. The author of the notice turned out to be the radio personality who is the voice behind the smiling vegetable giant. We spent the summer in his home, painting and working on our first magazine issue.

We chose the name *Post-American* because the magazine tried to put forward a Christian faith that broke free of the prevailing American civil religion. We described ourselves in our first issue as a movement from "two tribes"—student radicals who out of our commitment to justice discovered Jesus Christ as "an ally, a liberator, a Lord," and longtime Christians who began to see in the gospel a call to radical discipleship: "As radical Christians we seek to recover the earliest doctrines of Christianity, its historical basis, its radical ethical spirit, and its revolutionary consciousness. . . . Our small group has found itself to be part of an awakening, a volatile atmosphere, a movement of committed people who have found personal liberation and an ethical basis for social involvement in Jesus, as revealed in the New Testament documents, and the ability to live that life in the Spirit of God. . . . We dedicate ourselves to no ideology, government, or system, but to active obedience to our Lord and His Kingdom, and to sacrificial service to the people for whom he died."

The magazine became a vehicle for creating a communication network and information clearinghouse for "radical Christians" around the country, by providing resources about the abuse of American power and the necessity of Christian response.

We printed thirty thousand copies of that first issue, a sixteen-page tabloid, but we had no mailing list. We began to brainstorm names of people we thought might be sympathetic to what we were trying to say. Some of us decided that we would travel around the country, some going east and some west, carrying the *Post-American* to colleges, seminaries, churches, and receptive individuals along the way.

The price of a subscription for four issues over the first year was "two dollars or whatever you can afford." We had decided that we wouldn't put out another issue until enough money came back to pay for the first and print a second.

Later we would learn how important that early financial decision had been. It meant that we would be financially independent and never have to rely on any organization, foundation, denomination, or wealthy donors. We would put out the magazine only if its readers would continue to pay for it. That principle has endured.

From the beginning, the *Post-American* defied categorization. Evangelicals could see that our faith was clearly biblical and orthodox, but our social and political understanding of the gospel fundamentally challenged the evangelical world view. The *Post-American* also mystified religious liberals, for here was a publication more theologically orthodox and conservative than they were, proclaiming a far more radical political stance.

The relationship between the members of our little group was the foundation for the publication of the magazine, though during our first year together we would never have called ourselves a community or even thought of that as a goal. The magazine gave a focus to our relationship, a task around which we gathered, and the excitement of new ideas soon became the catalyst for thoughts about a community.

We made ourselves aware of the long and broad historical tradition of Christian communities committed to radical discipleship. Just as we had learned that we were not alone in the present, we were finding that throughout Christian history all the convictions and commitments that were beginning to shape our life had been present in the lives of other believers. We began to see that Christian radicalism was not something that grew out of our heads, but out of the life we shared together. After that first summer, we decided to continue living together.

In the fall of 1971, we moved into Lake Bluff, another Chicago suburb. Our house was easily identifiable; it was the white frame one next to the sewer, with the bright yellow school buses parked out front. We kept up seminary work, drove buses for special education children in the early mornings and afternoons, and put out the *Post-American* quarterly.

The house quickly became a gathering point for other people, most of whom were seminary students. By that time, our group had grown to include single women and married couples. We worshiped together and discussed the magazine and other possibilities for ministry.

We felt that to talk of the church meant to talk of community, although our understanding of that was very immature and embryonic. Those of us who had once talked of rejecting the church began to talk about new ways of being the church. Out of these discussions grew a desire to make the commitment to the poor and their struggles that we articulated so strongly in the magazine a focus of our life together. We moved in the fall of 1972 into two adjoining apartments a block from Lake Michigan in the Rogers Park area, just above Howard Street, a low-income section of north Chicago.

The apartments had inadequate heat, so that in the winter we got accustomed to eating dinner in our parkas and having late-night conversations in the kitchen around the open oven. The *Post-American* was put together on an enclosed porch, where winds came blasting off the lake, a numbing experience for much of the year, requiring the ability to type while wearing gloves.

Our two years there marked a gradual erosion of our relationships to one another. The "common enemy" of an alienating seminary experience that had held us together was replaced by a sense of common mission in the city. But as we worked together, we began to disagree over making that mission specific.

A long process of fragmentation was underway. As we tried to talk specifically about what it was we were committing ourselves to, our discussions turned into arguments over what model of community we would create. We would pick and choose aspects of communities with which we were familiar, hoping with a great deal of pride to create a model community unlike any other in existence.

As our egos became more and more involved, the discussions became increasingly competitive, and the talks turned into a forum for working out our personal conflicts and identity stuggles. We were in reality more a collective of people than a community, very ideological about our life and how it would be shaped.

Our desire to conceptualize a model for community dominated our concerns and conversations and eclipsed our love and care for one another. We believed that the key to community was finding the best structure for it, and our preoccupation with creating the perfect model substituted for the quality of our relationships to each other. The increasing conflict and hurt built a spirit of self-destruction among us.

We had thought that we had found some truth, but it wasn't

working. We lost our innocence about community, and then began to lose faith and hope. We had moved into the city with high expectations, but found ourselves mired in a two-year deterioration of our life. We were not only unable to resolve differences among us about what our community would be, but, more basically, were unable to pull ourselves out of the distrust, hurt, and betrayal we felt toward one another.

Finally we formally dissolved the bonds and commitments that had been between us and moved into new living situations and in different directions. The great experiment had failed.

Some of us still felt affection and friendship for one another, so a few small clusters remained intact. Many of us moved into different apartments in another poor area of Chicago called Uptown, where Joe Roos and I were the magazine's only staff for several months. Even during this time, the *Post-American* had a ministry in people's lives all over the country, but those of us directly involved felt an increasing despair about the shape and direction of our work.

I remember going out on speaking trips conscious of the fragmentation and growing disintegration of our life together back home, and feeling myself to have less and less to say to other people. On a few occasions I frankly admitted what I felt. In the middle of one speech, I stopped to say that the words were hollow to me, that my spirit was broken and hurting, and all I could do was invite people to come up where we could sit together and talk about our struggles, fears, and hopes.

Our concern for the "big" issues, the prophetic witness, had overwhelmed our coming to terms with the most basic things: whether we were loving one another, serving one another, laying down our lives for one another as we were talking about the church laying down its life for the sake of the world. The distance between our concern for healing and justice in the world and those same concerns for one another in the life we shared was a wide gulf.

In our apartment of five we didn't talk of community or even use the word anymore. We had thought that we could create this thing with our own resources and ideas, and we had failed.

I had never before felt so completely depleted of resources and strength. For the first time, I found that I couldn't come up with an answer. Trying to think of one only brought up all the feelings of frustration and despair.

We all felt anger, blaming each other, blaming God, questioning that the call we had felt had even been real. But then the anger gave way to an intense feeling of our own failure and sin, each of us aware of how our pride and intellectualizing had prevented community from occurring among us. That awareness forced each one to cry out to God out of the poverty of our own spirits.

Like the others, I was overcome with a desperate need to turn to God in a way that I never had before. And in our desperation, God turned us back to one another. We began simply to pray together.

Our confidence had been so strong that we had to be broken down to nothing before anything could be rebuilt. We were broken so that God could begin to work among us. When we had been controlling everything, there was no room for God's Spirit to work.

As each of us examined our faith, we began to learn how to forgive one another. Each of us, in tentative ways at first, went to the others to confess our sin. Out of the tearful healing of broken relationships, a new worship experience grew up, and the broken bonds of trust were repaired.

At the time, some of us were reading Dietrich Bonhoeffer's *Life Together*. One part of the book hadn't made sense to us until that experience: he had written that our own vision of what we were going to be as a community needed first to be shattered, and that shattering was God's grace. When we began to throw away our agendas, we started thinking about one another—a crucial change. When we stopped thinking about being a community, we began to be one.

A number of the married couples decided to form a community in a rural setting in Michigan's upper peninsula, which became Menominee River Fellowship. Other people had simply left, abandoning not only community but in some cases their faith. Their leaving was difficult for us.

But it is clear now that God was redeeming that time of failure and crisis for us and had nurtured us, not in spite of it, but because of it. We all found a deeper trust in God and one another; and in the struggle and resulting reconciliation were the seeds of a new community.

In the beginning of 1975, other people were drawn to us (including my sister, Barb, and her husband, Jim Tamialis). Knowing that people wanted to join the life that was growing among us was deeply confirming. New life began to blossom in Uptown.

But other new life was coming to Uptown as well—developers and renovators who were displacing our low-income neighbors from their homes. The entire north side of Chicago was beginning to be "gentrified"—transformed into upper-income housing—and it looked to us that we had little future in the neighborhood.

We felt the need to move, both for the purpose of continuing our proximity to the poor, and because we sensed a need to establish this "new thing" happening among us in some new place. We had learned that we didn't resolve all of our questions by discussion, so we decided to pray about where and how this new life would come about. Our prayer and waiting lasted six months.

During that time some of us visited the Church of the Redeemer in Houston, Texas, an Episcopal parish that had experienced a renewal of its life under the ministry of Graham Pulkingham. Our time there convinced us that we had to be as committed to the pastoral dimension of our life as to the prophetic. We came away feeling that both vision and nurture were critical for the survival of any community. Without a gospel vision of justice for the world, community can become ingrown and self-serving; and without nurturing relationships, community does not exist, as we knew only too well. We were ready to try again with a hope of more integration of the two dimensions of our life.

We knew we wanted to leave Chicago. We considered going to the West Coast, but it seemed too far away from family and friends. We all started to lean toward coming East, especially since more of the new connections and friendships we were developing through the *Post-American* were east of us rather than west of us. Philadelphia seemed like the best place, with Washington, D.C., as a possible second choice. There were good friends, communities, and churches with kindred spirits in both places.

We gathered for a weekend of prayer and discernment in Chicago, with friends from both Philadelphia and Washington. I don't recall any intense discussion that weekend, and certainly no arguments; by the end of the time, everyone simply felt that Washington was the right place for us to move.

The big drawback of Washington was that it is the nation's capital and the center of political power, and we didn't want to be in the middle of all that. But we decided to come anyway and live in one of the poor sections of the city. It often amuses me when people think that the reason we came to Washington, like most everyone else here, was to be closer to the center of power, when in reality that fact almost kept us from coming.

Four of us came to Washington for a few days to look for housing. On the last day of our search we found two houses side by side in a low-income neighborhood. We had a new home.

In the fall of 1975, eighteen adults, two babies, a puppy, and a cat moved to Washington to begin a new life together. Some of the others were not as enthralled as we had been over our housing find. The interior of one of the houses was painted entirely in "swimming pool green" and filled with broken-down furniture, old mattresses, and piles of plaster. For several weeks while we fixed up that house, all twenty of us shared our meals around one table in the other. But a feeling of hope and joy pervaded even the most arduous of our settling-in tasks.

Our faith was being rekindled in the power of love. An almost inexplicable sense of commitment and call to give ourselves to the new life among us was taking hold of Bob Sabath, his wife, Jackie, and myself. Our relationship, coupled with a commitment to a pastoral life, became the ground for the leadership that emerged within the fellowship during our first weeks in Washington.

Our experience in Chicago had shown us that we needed to have leadership that was explicit and affirmed by everyone in the community, as well as tenderly exercised and held accountable to the responsibilities it was given. We worked to establish a form of leadership that was patterned after the biblical model of servanthood, that was given authority in a context of trust and mutual submission, that did not seek control but nurtured others into spiritual maturity.

Resolving our questions about leadership was just one part of a process of community identity formation. The group, no longer defined solely by the magazine, branched out into ministry in the neighborhood, including youth and housing work.

We sought to develop an economic life that was both biblically sound and politically responsible. The teachings and life of Jesus displayed a profound identification with the poor, and we came to see that to live simply was as much a spiritual necessity as it was a political one. Scriptural imperatives demanded that we break from the societal patterns of overconsumption and waste that helped perpetuate global exploitation.

We also wanted to be accountable to one another economically, so that we were not making economic choices in isolation. We saw that our desire to share with one another economically was a sign of our sharing on other levels.

We read in the second and fourth chapters of Acts that the coming of the Holy Spirit among the believers had shattered the old economic assumptions and created among them a new economic order that was marked by a new generosity toward one another and the poor. Inspired by their witness, we set up a pattern of economic sharing in which all of our money was pooled and then paid out for rent, food, and other expenses, with an assumption of economic equality among us. We recognized that if justice and peace were to become the characteristics of the people of God, then our life together must reflect that justice and peace.

We have learned from many years in community that we have no more to give to the world than that which we have come to experience together. I understand more every day why Jesus identified our love for one another as the foundation of any ministry or witness that we have in the world. The healing of nations as biblically foreseen begins with the healing of our own lives, and people are deeply changed or nurtured only in an environment in which they feel loved.

At the center of that healing is worship. It is in worship that we find freedom in confession and forgiveness and receive the gift of reconciliation, the foundation of our life together. In the broken bread, Christ's frailty reminds us of our own, and his shed blood gives us a vision of the church's call to be poured out for the sake of the world. Around the Eucharist table we come again and again to be healed, reconciled, and sent forth whole.

It is in our worship that we come together to praise God and continually affirm our allegiance to his kingdom, denying the power of competing authorities. To be a community of Christians in our time is to be a community of resistance, but it is first of all to be a community of celebration. From our celebration flows our resistance.

We wanted the magazine to reflect the changes that we were undergoing, the things that we were discovering about ourselves and the church. What had begun as a barb in the conscience of establishment Christianity was taking on new dimensions. We wanted the magazine to show, both in spirit and name, the more affirming, upbuilding stance that we were feeling as a body of people. The name *Post-American* reflected, at best, a part of our identity.

It had become our conviction that more central than anything we do is who we are. The biblical tradition shows that God's purposes in history are carried primarily through the life of a people; and it is in the quality of the life they share and then lay down for the sake of the world that God's purposes of justice, peace, and liberation come to pass.

When we were still in Chicago, I had been reading Hebrews 11, which speaks of God's people as sojourners, or pilgrims. "Sojourners," I thought, would be a good name for the magazine. It expressed the identity of God's people as aliens who are citizens of another kingdom, fully present in the world but committed to a different order, those who learn to "sing the Lord's song in a strange land."

It was exactly that self-consciousness that the church in America needed to recover. Two days later, I got a postcard from Wes Michaelson, in Washington, D.C., who later became the managing editor of the magazine. It said simply: "An idea for the magazine's new name—Sojourners." After we came to Washington, we finally settled on the new name for both magazine and community.

We realized that building the body of Christ was not one of the many issues to which we were committed, as it once was, but the foundation for all that we do and are. The change to Sojourners reflected the deepening of our identity as a Christian community. We saw that the prophetic vocation was not only an attack on the old but offered a new vision for the church's life, which held the seeds of new possibilities in the wider society.

The magazine has come a long way from a sixteen-page tabloid run on a shoestring and out of a shoebox. The fourteen fists which appeared in the first issue of the *Post-American* have given way to a look and content more reflective of our deepening commitment to the church, to community and prayer, and of our growing ecumenical nature. But the magazine still retains the political analysis from a biblical perspective for which it was first known. *Sojourners* has been called radical and conservative, evangelical and catholic, activist and contemplative, personal and political, pastoral and prophetic.

Central to the magazine's vocation has been the integration

of things long divided, separated through the fragmentation of the church's life: evangelism and social justice, spirituality and politics, prayer and peacemaking, worship and action, faith and history.

Sojourners has always been a lot more than a magazine and less than an organization. It has been more like a very extended family with a growing kindred spirit, not only in our community but also in our circle of readers. Many find their way to visit us, keeping Janice Johnston, our guest coordinator, more than busy.

The magazine's readers hold meetings in cities and towns around the country, and out of those gatherings have come friendships, small groups for prayer and support, actions for peace and justice, new communities, and even marriages. Perhaps the most important thing they produce is hope.

There was a time when we felt a bit like a lonely voice crying in the wilderness. But now the desert is beginning to blossom. An awakening of Christian faith and conscience is apparent in many places.

Over the years, I think we've become more sure of the things we're committed to, but perhaps less self-righteous. We take our commitments even more seriously, but have learned to laugh more and take ourselves less seriously. We are more confident of the gospel, but more humble about our ability to live it out.

We are able to see not only the weakness and frailty of the church, but also the strength and hope that come from its history and present struggles. And over the years we have discovered the same weakness and hope in ourselves.

More and more at Sojourners, we see our role as simply calling people to faith, to a recovery of our commitment to Jesus Christ. The renewal of faith is finally the only thing with the strength to resist the economic and political powers, and to provide an adequate spiritual foundation for a more just way to live.

Our community, now numbering about forty people, serves

to call us also to faith. We see community as the environment for our continuing conversion.

After the first few years of any community's life, disillusionment sets in. For each of us the initial enthusiasm of beginning a community, or first joining one, gives way to daily routine. The romance wears off as we realize that the exciting experiment has become something that demands the commitment of our whole lives. Each of us faces the meaning of our choices and of being committed with very human people in not-so-extraordinary circumstances; yet the love, growth, freedom, and fulfillment of community can only be experienced as we make those commitments.

The choice for community means a choice against the leading values, rewards, and life patterns of our culture. Sometimes the power of the culture reasserts itself with new force, and the things we left joyfully behind to join community become attractive again, especially at crucial transition points like marriage, family, and vocational crisis. For a community's long-term survival against the assaults of the culture, at least two paths can be taken.

One would create an alternative system that protects people from the culture. Very strong, even rigid, corporate structures can be used to create an environment that is self-sufficient. Every community is tempted to find its security in structures which replace the securities offered by the society. But such structures can dominate, control, and stifle growth.

The second path creates a community environment that generates faith. The power of the culture is confronted primarily not by a community's structures but by the deepening faith of its members. This path requires more risk but produces greater maturity and truer security.

We seek to walk the second path, to live in such a way that our personal and corporate spiritual disciplines help us see and understand the movement of the Spirit in our inner lives, our community, the churches, and history. To sustain us over the years, our disciplines must not be used to protect us from the world or from one another, but to deepen our faith so that we can give more of our lives for the sake of Christ.

These disciplines include prayer, solitude, and spiritual direction. The relationship that each of us has with Jesus Christ is the building block of community, and that relationship needs to be affirmed and renewed in prayer. Millie Bender's vocation as a spiritual director among us has been crucial for anchoring ourselves in prayerful discipline, as she reminds us that all we do must be grounded in Christ and gently prods this community filled with the activities of ministry and family-raising to take time for retreat and solitude.

Bible study is also central to our life. As Dietrich Bonhoeffer's underground seminary did in Germany during World War II, we focus as a community on a scripture each week for personal meditation and Sunday worship.

We see also relationship to the poor as a spiritual discipline rather than simply an occasion for ministry. How much compassion we feel for our neighbors, rather than how much ministry we generate, should be the measure of our commitment. We've found that rest and play are also important, or our lives become simply a bundle of commitments. Over the long haul, humor and humility will be our saving graces.

Our fellowship together is both a gift and a demand, and both acceptance and loving confrontation are called for. Community is the context where both the love and the pain give life, and we move beyond sentimentality and judgment. Our spiritual disciplines and our vulnerability with one another can create an environment where vision, vitality, and creativity can flourish.

In chapter four of the second letter to the Corinthians, the apostle Paul describes a tremendous struggle of faith. I have often reflected over the years how his words have taken on more meaning as we have attempted to bring to birth a community of faith. It's very hard work, and it often feels like a kind of dying.

The pain of this birth struggle is felt emotionally, many times spiritually, and sometimes even physically. But the events of

June 12, 1982, made Paul's words more vivid for me than they have ever been before.

Jackie Sabath's contractions began early Friday morning. Her husband, Bob, came downstairs to my basement apartment to give me the news. My bag was packed, and I was ready to leave for New York to participate in the religious convocation being held in preparation for the peace march and rally there the next day. I unpacked my bag and stayed home.

The waiting began.

Julie Edgerton, one of the midwives and a longtime friend, came about four o'clock in the afternoon. Several of us from the community sat out on the porch together. It was funny to see that, as soon as the labor began, several people rushed home to make food: chicken, brownies, and pie. We were well fed throughout the entire event.

In the early evening, Jackie went upstairs to stay. It was the beginning of a very long and hard night. Community people began to come and gather in the living room downstairs. Together we kept the vigil that continued through the birth.

The house felt really blessed that night, filled with love, support, and fervent intercession. The lowest point came about four in the morning. Jackie had been very strong and brave through the whole thing, but the pain had been growing for hours. She and Bob were very weary and had become discouraged.

Julie told us how hard it was going, and we gathered to pray. Only a short time later Bob came running down with a smile on his face to say that the water had broken and the baby was coming. Martha Kincannon, reflecting on our prayer, said, "We should have done this about three hours ago."

We all gathered at the foot of the stairs where we could hear everything: Jackie's cries, Julie's encouragement, and the instructions of the midwives—"Easy, Jackie, easy. Blow, blow." We all blew.

Then we heard the delighted exclamation. "It's a girl! It's a girl!" and an amazing sound—the baby's first cry. Suddenly we had the sensation of a new person upstairs. It was a very emotional moment for all of us. There wasn't a dry eye in the house.

Just as the first cry came, I looked out the window and saw that it was just getting light. After the long, long night, Kathryn Claire had come with the dawn.

Paul talks about the treasure we have in earthen vessels. I realized that Saturday morning that Jackie was indeed an earthen vessel. The treasure was new life—new life in the image of God.

Paul speaks of being persecuted and struck down, but never forsaken. We are given up to death so that the life of Jesus may be manifested in us.

I read these verses after the birth and pictured Jackie's labor. I thought of her faithfulness through it. And now, when I hold Claire, I value her with a sense of awe and joy at the realization that this beautiful child is the fruit of much labor and pain.

The experience has helped me understand what is going on in each of us and among us as a community. I have a vivid image of God among us indeed like a mother in labor, enduring pain and, I would venture, long hours of discouragement. And God remains faithful until those moments of birth that take place in each of us.

That evening I told Jackie that three-quarters of a million people had marched for peace in New York. She was very glad and excited and watched attentively the reports on T.V. There was no need for anyone to draw connections between the events in New York and the events that night in our home. She knew, and was grateful for all who marched, because they were marching for Claire.

The same day hundreds of thousands of people filled the streets of New York, a baby was born at Sojourners. Both events were for the same cause—the continuing of life. "Choose life," said the writer of Deuteronomy, "that you and your descendants may live."

There is no birth without labor, no life without death, says Paul. It is the oldest pattern we know, and it is acted out again and again among us. Paul says that it is also the pattern of life and growth for Christians and the church.

For me, there is a new image in all this. It is an image of each of us, all of us, being invited to join in the labor of God for the sake of the world. Jackie's labor was also the labor of God; there was something deeply divine in every step and every stage. Somehow she was a part of God's labor, and God's labor was a part of her.

We too have joined the labor of God, the labor for life, for justice, and for peace. They won't come with a decisive act, or a march, or an event, but very likely it will take a long night of labor and struggle to bring to birth a day of new and better possibilities. We will no doubt get discouraged and feel like giving up. But in the morning, as on the Saturday morning of June 12 when Kathryn Claire was born, life will always come to us again.

Washington, D.C., has for eight years been the home where our life has deepened and new vision has been forged. When asked in 1975 why we chose to move here, our reasons were never very clear. (Gentrification proved to be worse in Washington, D.C., than it had been in Chicago.) At that time, we felt simply that we were being called to this city.

But Washington has turned out to be an important environment for the maturing of our life. The juxtaposition of making community among the poor and powerless while confronting those in places of power has deepened our convictions to live a life in the service of justice.

6
A Tale of Two Cities

Washington, D.C., is actually two cities inhabiting the same territory. There is official Washington, the city everyone knows, the capital of the United States of America. It is a place of monuments, marble, and malls. Stately and cold, the proud architecture of government buildings proclaims this to be the locus of all that is important.

The official city's chief characteristic and commodity is power. People are here because they have it, want it, or just like to be close to it. Here are the powerful, the power hungry, and the power groupies.

But there is another Washington. It is a city that few know. The people who live here are mostly black and poor. Their neighborhoods are only blocks from the government buildings, but they might as well be a thousand miles away. There are no monuments here, just substandard housing. Broken glass is far more common than marble. Here, the kids don't play on grassy malls; they run up and down dirty streets and rat-infested alleys.

This city is a center of things too: things like unemployment, drugs, alcohol, crime, and despair. The leading characteristic of this other Washington is powerlessness.

The black population of the District of Columbia historically has served as the domestic help and cheap labor pool for those who run the government. Colonialism is still the best word to describe the tale of these two cities. The seven hundred thousand residents of the District don't even have the right to send voting members to Congress, where the social priorities of the nation are determined.

For years now, that Congress has decided to allocate more than half the nation's public monies to the military, and the amount increases every year. Cries for a balanced budget and more military spending come in the same breath. As always, the money is being taken away from social programs, which lack the powerful lobbies of the Pentagon and military contractors to defend them.

The nation has decided that the poor will bear the burden of budget-balancing acts. The Pentagon spends and wastes more, but social programs are an easy target. Those programs usually serve more to control poor people than to establish justice, and they are often inefficient. The poor don't like them. No one likes them. But until we have some alternatives, poor people suffer as the food stamps dry up in our neighborhood; as welfare benefits and job-training programs are cut back; and as legal services, health clinics, and day-care centers close their doors.

From the vantage point of official Washington, the overriding issue is staying ahead of the Russians militarily. But the discussion over budget priorities looks very different from the vantage point of the other Washington. People aren't worried about staying ahead of the Russians here, they're worried about surviving the harsh realities of being poor in the United States. They don't perceive their enemies to be in Moscow, but in Washington's corridors of power.

There is already a war being waged against the poor. Precious resources are being robbed to feed the engines of war. When the government tightens its belt, it does so around the necks of the poor. And so far, the nation has accepted this policy.

By every major index of urban life, conditions have worsened since the riots of the sixties. A whole class of desperate people live in our cities with no hope, no future, and no stake in this country. Many of them are young, and they are full of rage.

Our community makes its home in the 14th Street "riot corridor," one of the sections of Washington that burned during the riots following the assassination of Martin Luther King, Jr. Some people who were here during those riots say the feeling on the street today is much the same as it was then. The people in our neighborhood feel under assault by the priorities of a government that has labeled them expendable.

Violence and desperation stalk the forgotten neighborhoods of cities like ours. There has been little public attention, let alone public outcry, over the oppression of America's poor. There is little concern that murder is now the primary cause of death for young, black males; that drug abuse among the poor has increased by tremendous proportions since the 1960s; that many ghetto schools no longer pretend to teach but turn out graduates who can neither read nor write; that four of ten black students in those schools will not get jobs; that police often simply contain or tolerate urban crime unless the victims are white; and that the unemployment and impoverishment of a whole class of people is regarded as an acceptable cost of the economic system.

The murders of twenty-six black children in Atlanta in 1981 riveted our attention for a few months, but concern about the underlying causes of the murders was largely buried as soon as a suspect was captured. The real issue for Atlanta's black children, and all black people, is the vulnerability of a people forced to live on the margins of a society that still refuses to grant them the most basic requirements of human dignity and justice. The nature of life in Atlanta's poorest sections made those twenty-six children easy prey, and made stopping the killing extremely difficult.

Ironically, the integration of educated black people into the middle class has in some ways negatively affected the poor black community. The concept of the "new black middle class" has proven quite attractive to the media and to whites generally. It allows America to feel that its racial problems are mostly solved and blinds most whites to the continued poverty and hopelessness of the masses of black people.

Statistics have been manipulated, definitions of middle-class status lowered a bit, and blacks have become more visible in advertising and the media, all serving to create the impression that the black middle class is larger and more secure than it really is. But even blacks who have jobs are losing ground to their white counterparts. Labor Department reports show a growing gap between white and black incomes, with wages for whites increasing at twice the rate of those for blacks.

The system remains intact, having again shown its power to resist or co-opt any basic change, and having gained greater credibility by adding black faces without making fundamental alterations in its structure and purposes. Even most whites who were once allies of the civil rights movement have gone on to other issues and concerns.

Blacks now struggle for economic justice, and that battle is much more threatening than marching for legal desegregation. For most blacks the issue is still survival. Political gains are not enough when economic servitude continues to be the principal fact of life.

We have been in our neighborhood long enough to see black children grow into teen-agers. We have seen the promise of youth wasted by the hard facts of growing up without hope for the future. This too is violence against children, but it isn't an issue for most white Americans.

The last time I checked black youth unemployment in Washington, D.C., the official figure was 61 percent. The real rate of unemployment is always higher; in my observation only about one in four kids has a job. Many have already quit school. Others stay but wonder why they should when they know there won't be any work for them after graduation. The value of an education is harder and harder to explain to kids.

The suffering of those on the bottom is the biblical measure of any society. The growing unemployment rate is a strong indictment of America. Now hovering at the highest level since the Depression, unemployment is a cruel and sinful waste of human resources and lives. The masses of jobless people are human testimony to our nation's lack of political will and imagination and compassion.

To many the highest unemployment in forty-two years is simply a negative milestone in history, but in our neighborhood, it represents a new depth of suffering for our friends.

Under the Reagan administration, the official neglect of the poor is sanctioned and even justified in the name of sound fiscal policy. The poor are always made to pay for the sins of the rest of society. Always.

White racism is this country's oldest and deepest sin. We have yet to come to terms with it and the way it has poisoned our national life and corrupted the American spirit. And it begins to claim its victims while they are still children. Some of those children have been our best teachers about the nature of the two Washingtons.

When we first pulled up in our U-Haul truck from Chicago in the fall of 1975, they were there playing in the street and sitting on the stoops of the two houses that were to be our new homes. The delegation of kids was not the standard Washington welcoming committee, but then we weren't exactly a group of visiting foreign dignitaries either.

The kids immediately jumped up and offered to unload the truck. With boundless energy, they helped us with the ritual of transferring armloads of stuff from truck to home. They showed a particular interest in the old mattresses that had inhabited the houses, and soon we were helping them move a pile of them to a collection of mattresses they kept stashed in the alley at the end of the block. We learned later its significance.

Most of the kids were from two families who lived down the street in a two-flat house. Eleven Williams kids, all under fourteen years of age, shared a one-bedroom apartment with their parents, and five Joneses shared a similar one with their mother. The Williams family especially worked its way quickly into our lives.

The kids were around our households most of the time, and before long we were regularly involved with them in the afternoons after school. Soon the word spread around the neighborhood, and we developed a full-fledged after-school program of recreation and tutoring for about two dozen kids.

The trips we took together were the favorite part of the program. Most of the kids had never been to Washington's monuments, its art galleries, or museums. They had never before ventured into official Washington's world of powerful people and white tourists. They were wide-eyed at the view from the top of the Washington Monument and at the treasures they discovered at the Smithsonian Institution.

Trips to the country, the seashore, the mountains were filled with adventure—from campfires to jellyfish stings. We soon learned about the fears that overnight camping brought to kids who on their own turf had learned to be tough. Used to fending off rats and cockroaches, they worried about being eaten by squirrels and rabbits. The quiet of the mountains was unfamiliar and frightening—no comforting sounds of home, like sirens, shouts in the night, and shattering glass.

But the activity that occupied most of the Williams kids' time had to do with their treasure trove of mattresses. One day they invited us to the alley, where they had laid all the mattresses end to end. Broken-down and dirty easy chairs the kids had found in a trash heap were assembled into a row of seats for our viewing pleasure. One after another, from the oldest to the youngest, the kids came running down the alley, hit the mattresses, and performed an amazing array of backflips, somersaults, and handsprings. They called themselves the "Afrobats."

We were astounded at the skill of some of the kids, especially the oldest, Earl. He was the teacher, coach, and main event. His younger brothers and sisters and other neighborhood kids were learning well under his instruction. After they finished their routine and received our standing ovation, they surrounded us, wanting to know what we thought of their tricks.

Our enthusiasm and appreciation spurred them on, and eventually led us to call a local T.V. news crew to come out and film the back-alley gymnasts. The thrill of performing for T.V. cameras was enough to make any kid do backflips, and they did them well. The news department was equally excited at the discovery of new inner-city sports talent.

For the next year Earl trained hard, working long hours after school in the high school gymnasium to perfect his routine. He went on to win the city gymnastics tournament two years in a row. There was a time when talk circulated of a college scholarship and an Olympic tryout. Some of the others also won a number of trophies, and the Williams brothers became well known as a class act in inner-city Washington.

The three youngest children—preschoolers—were unable to be involved in the after-school program and a bit too young to be counted among the "Afrobats," so a program to meet their needs was developed. Barb Tamialis, with two infants of her own, was already involved in full-time day-care with children. After a fire struck a rooming house two doors away, she visited the building and discovered three other young children in need of care during the day. The eight children became the focus of a day-care program which grew into an organized play and learning experience in the basement of one of our households and then the living room of the other.

Washington's housing crisis hit home one day when Lil Williams, the kids' mother, walked down to our house with an eviction notice she had received. She had paid her rent, but her landlord was evicting her in order to renovate and sell the house at a large profit. That day gave us the first inkling of a pattern that would be repeated again and again in our experience in Washington.

The eviction notice gave Lil and her family thirty days to vacate their house. She didn't know what to do, and neither did we. We went to work researching the situation, finding out about the law, eviction procedures, the rights of landlords and tenants. We discovered that she had been threatened with eviction without due process, and we convinced her to fight her landlord in court.

Mrs. Jones, her distrust and fear of the system too great,

couldn't be talked into coming down to the courthouse with us. She simply packed up her family and left, as so many poor families do.

The courtroom scene is still vivid in my memory. Perk Perkins and I went down with Lil and sat next to her, one on each side. We had talked with her at length about her rights and options and told her we were prepared to back her all the way.

The courtroom was filled with more than a hundred people who were facing eviction. They were all black; the judges and lawyers were all white. All the tenants were being evicted by the same group of landlords, who were all in turn represented by the same law firm.

The landlord's lawyer wandered through the room offering cash settlements to those who would forfeit their rights and quietly leave their apartments. The money was less than the cost of a security deposit on a new apartment, but the tenants were afraid, knowing that they would ultimately lose their homes anyway. All except Lil took what small amount of cash they were offered.

The crowd was called to stand around the judge's bench, and the judge asked them if they knew that the paper they had just signed was a surrender of their legal rights in this matter and that they would have to leave their homes. They all said that they understood. The case was settled, and they walked out of the courtroom robbed of homes and dignity, with nothing but a small sum of money to show for their day in court.

Lil, Perk, and I approached the bench. She said simply, "Judge, I want my rights." No sooner had the words come out than the lawyer said, "Your honor, we withdraw our case." Having failed to evict her illegally, the landlord could wait for the legal process to run its course and eventually remove Lil and her family. Though we had only bought time, we, Lil, and the kids felt like it had been a victory. Most important in the experience was the feeling of being in this fight together, a feeling that would become very familiar.

A few weeks later, I passed by their home and found Ronnie,

one of the boys, sitting on the stoop looking angry and sullen. "I'm gonna get me a gun," he said, "I'm gonna get me a gun."

"Why do you want a gun?" I asked him.

"A rat crawled over Boochie's face in bed last night. I wanna get me a gun and kill that old rat."

With winter coming on, the Williams house was literally overtaken by rats, scrambling to get in out of the cold. As brazen as they were ugly, the rats had staked their claim on the house and leered at anyone who caught them on a kitchen countertop or under a bed.

A few of us arrived one day with boots and baseball bats to try to clear them out. It was my first rat hunt; there would be others. There were so many places of arrival and exit in the house that the rats were impossible to corner. They accomplished what the landlord couldn't, and the Williamses began to search for another place to live.

With little time to look, and no place immediately available, six of us decided to share a house with them. Earl, Theresa, Charlie, Wesley, Ronnie, Boochie, Melissa, Janice, Anthony, Leon, Isaac, Lil, Fred, and the six of us moved into a five-bedroom house, along with their huge part-German Shepherd mongrel, Champ, whose large incisors and nasty temper earned him the nickname around the neighborhood of "Chomp."

I will never forget our first dinner together. Exterminators had set off roach bombs earlier that day. Just as I was about to pray over the meal, cockroaches began to fall one by one from the ceiling on to our table, which community members had specially built according to huge specifications. All at once, kids started popping up out of their chairs, smashing the bugs with a smack of the palm and a "Gotcha!"

We were a strange family indeed for six months. To feed the crew at breakfast required three dozen eggs, or seventy pancakes, and a traffic director to keep a minimum of half the kids out of the way of the cook.

We encountered two major problems. One was laundry, which was a nonstop chore. We went through a box of detergent every few days.

The other was the bathroom problem—we had only two. Every morning the ritual was the same. By 7:30 long lines had formed, and by 7:32 four-year-old Leon would holler from the back, "I gots to pee!"

In the process of living so crowded together, we got very close. The kids helped with cooking, dishes, and shopping. We played ball together and helped them with their schoolwork. We knew that they eventually needed to be a family on their own again, but the friendships we established in that house have been built on over the years. They eventually found a house in an adjacent neighborhood. When the plague of gentrification asserted itself strongly in our neighborhood, we moved over to theirs.

The next year they were burned out of their home in the new neighborhood. Like many families who can't afford to pay their heating bills, they tried to keep the house warm in winter by turning on their oven and opening its door, as well as overusing space heaters, which are often old and electrically faulty. This system isn't very successful, serving only to create houses that are simultaneously cold and fire hazards. It was a blanket against a space heater that caused the fire that left them homeless again.

For two months some of the kids moved back into our households. Then they found a new home in the southeast quadrant of Washington, in the opposite corner of the city. Although we don't see them as often anymore, the older ones sometimes come back to visit.

Things never worked out for Earl. His family's multitude of problems helped undermine his discipline and enthusiasm. All of his gymnastics trophies and ribbons were destroyed in the fire, and with them his only source of pride. Despite our efforts to convince him of the importance of his education, he still hasn't finished high school.

Earl has slipped into the directionless despair that claims the lives of so many black teen-agers, while his best athletic years and the dream of a better future slip through his fingers. He was the subject of a front-page *Washington Post* article in 1981 which bore the headline, "Aspiring Gymnast's Dream Falters." It was the story of a talented kid who was done in by the pressures of the inner city.

In the eight years we have lived in Washington, the Williams family has moved five times. They are a textbook case of the problems that the poor face in our inner cities. There is never enough money or food. Housing and medical care are always inadequate.

Not one of the kids has finished high school, and it is doubtful that any will. The older kids, having dropped out of school, are unemployed or underemployed. At least one of the boys already has a serious drug and alcohol problem. The oldest girl, still a teen-ager, recently had a baby.

But they are more than a textbook case; they are real people who were our first friends in Washington. Watching the continual litany of their problems and being for the most part powerless to bring any change has been a painful education about the oppressive conditions under which the poor must learn to survive.

Their first home, now cleared of its army of rats, is a beautifully renovated townhouse. A professional white couple resides where two large families used to live, their home a monument in this city of monuments to the influence of power and money.

The couple is part of a new movement of people called the "urban pioneers," the first wave of the back-to-the-city phenomenon that is transforming our nation's inner cities. While government officials, real estate developers, the national media, and the returning middle class sing the praises of urban rejuvenation, the painful cost of redevelopment is being borne by the poor residents of inner-city neighborhoods that have suddenly become fashionable and profitable. In the hectic swirl of powerful economic interests, confusing public policies, and competing political values, the lives of poor people end up getting the lowest priority.

In our neighborhood, Columbia Heights, the price of unrestored homes rose from an average of $15,000 in 1975 to

$110,000 in 1980. Many apartment dwellings have been reconverted to single-family townhouses and condominiums. In large, multi-unit buildings which cannot be converted, rents are skyrocketing. Many observers predict that by 1984, 200,000 Washingtonians will have been displaced, either priced out of their apartments or left homeless as rental units vanish from the market.

Homeless people are not unusual in Washington. Very soon after we arrived in the city we became involved with Washington's "street people." Many are chronic alcoholics, drug addicts, patients released from mental institutions. All have problems in addition to being poor; most suffer emotional or physical disabilities. Some are veterans who never recovered from the war. Some even work but cannot make enough money to pay Washington's exorbitant rents. What they share is the fact that they have no place to stay, nowhere to go.

Their situation becomes especially vulnerable during the winter months when they face the possibility of freezing to death on the street, as some have every year since we've been in Washington. They die of exposure in abandoned buildings, alleyways, in the parks a stone's throw from government buildings, and even on the steps of churches.

One of the most pathetic and ironic sights in Washington, which brings home the contrast of power and powerlessness in Washington's two cities in a most dramatic way, is that of men and women sleeping during bitter cold nights on the steam grates outside places such as the Washington Monument, the Watergate Hotel, the State Department, the Department of Justice. Here they get the benefit of the exhaust from the heating systems that warm the government buildings. But the dangers of serious burns, or pneumonia from the combination of moisture and cold night air, are always present.

We have joined with other community groups in the city to provide "night hospitality" for street people. During our first winters in D.C. we cruised the streets in vans at night to gather up people from their steam grates, from bus stations and street corners, to carry them to two local churches that opened up their basements to provide overnight shelter. Some of the people preferred the solitude of a cold night over the crowded shelters, and with them we left a sandwich and a hot baked potato.

One man had made himself a home in a deserted parking garage. A card table covered with old army blankets was his shelter, and twenty-five crates of stale, flat biscuits he found discarded behind the FBI building—stored there for years for use in fallout shelters in the case of a nuclear attack—were his sustenance.

We took turns staffing the overnight shelters and providing meals. These were long nights of conversation and trouble-shooting, punctuated occasionally by a few minutes of sleep, but more often by heated arguments among the patrons.

The first year more than 1,100 churches, synagogues, and mosques were contacted about space for overnight shelter use, but only two responded. Community groups eventually put pressure on the District of Columbia government to open up some public shelters, which are far from ideal, but a hopeful step. A broad, church-based coalition was formed to deal with the problems of Washington's homeless.

But the existence of such people within the borders of the capital city of the world's richest nation still seems hard to believe. Their presence is ignored by the people in power, whose buildings are often their campground.

Most of Washington's chronically homeless people are a rare breed, made fiercely independent from their life on the streets. But now their ranks are being swelled by the victims of Washington's housing crisis. They are people who have never been on the street before, but now have to learn to survive this brutal existence. Most families can find relatives and friends to double or triple up with, but some people find themselves with no one and no place.

In the name of physical and fiscal revitalization, the displacement of the poor to make room for the rich is creating a desperate class of urban refugees. Piles of furniture and belongings on the curb, the signs of eviction, are commonplace in our neighborhood.

Carried out by federal marshalls, the process of eviction in the District of Columbia is especially callous. If the about-to-be-evicted family isn't at home, marshalls break in and move all the furnishings and personal belongings out on to the street. The doors are padlocked, and a sign put up warning that anyone trying to reenter will be legally prosecuted. Imagine the feeling of coming home at night to find yourself locked out, legally barred from entering, and all your possessions—those that haven't already been looted—on the curb.

The process is entirely legal and completely heartless. The only concession to compassion is that the marshalls will not evict on a rainy day.

We learned in the fall of 1978 that the house across the street from where we were living had been sold to real estate speculators, who were initiating a process to evict the six families who resided there. Katherine, one of the building's tenants, having heard that we were involved in people's housing problems, came to us for help. We investigated the situation and discovered that the two new owners had bought the building for $50,000 and were planning to sell it a few months later without improvements for $90,000, close to a 100 percent profit.

We went to the owners and offered to buy the building at the price they paid for it. We planned to place it into a neighborhood-owned trust, so that its residents could stay in their homes. The owners refused, reaffirming their intention to evict all the residents and sell the building for a handsome profit.

All the tenants except Katherine quietly left. We decided on a public course of action to bring attention to what was happening to inner-city residents like these, victimized by a rapidly expanding real estate market and ruthless speculation. We placed a $10,000 down payment on the building in an escrow account, then assumed ownership in the name of the trust.

On a Friday afternoon in September, we held a rally at the building, a celebration of neighborhood ownership. Katherine shattered a bottle of Champale against an outside wall of her home while the rest of us cheered. Her two-year-old son, Ofon, attended our community's day-care center. His young classmates carried signs as tall as they were proclaiming, "Let Ofon Keep His Home," and then planted two young trees on the front lawn.

Then, in a symbolic move, five of us entered the house with our mattresses and toothbrushes, and a blanket or two, to begin an occupation of the vacant apartments and "take up residence" in our new home. We waited through the night for the response of the owners.

Very early Saturday morning, seven police cars accompanying two police wagons pulled up in front of the house. We were arrested, handcuffed, and taken off to the D.C. jail. A crowd gathered to witness the arrest scene. Our community's children showed up in their pajamas, and a neighbor, thinking he was witnessing a standard eviction, said, "If you need a place to stay, I can help."

We spent the weekend in jail. At our arraignment, one lawyer suggested we plead insanity, since "anyone who thinks they can fight speculation in D.C. is crazy." Though we lost the battle for that building, the action seemed to galvanize attention and action around the housing problems of the poor, particularly in the city's Christian community, and Katherine and her family moved in with us for several months.

The action taught us some valuable lessons. We learned that providing hospitality for evicted families wasn't enough. We also learned that symbolic actions like the one we had undertaken are of little value unless people are getting organized in their buildings and neighborhoods, and are being empowered themselves to deal with their housing problems.

That event and reflection on it sparked a new direction in our housing work, and we began to think about tenant organizing. In the fall of 1978 we held meetings with the Community of Hope, a Nazarene church located a few blocks away, to discuss the housing crisis in our neighborhood.

After several meetings, a clear consensus emerged that any new involvement in housing would have to address the central cause of displacement: lack of power in the poor community. The decisions that had brought about the housing crisis had been made by bankers, real estate brokers, developers, and city officials, all removed from Columbia Heights. The economic system had successfully marginalized, isolated, and disenfranchised the poor.

We became convinced that if we wanted to help we must commit ourselves to ministry that serves to empower the poor. Our hope was that the tenants of Columbia Heights, organized together, could become a political force that would challenge and change the housing trends that cause displacement.

We started small with three organizers, Perk Perkins, David McKeithen, and Jim Tamialis, in a few buildings in January of 1979. Within a year, tenant leadership began to emerge and establish direction in ten buildings. In the spring of 1980, tenants from these buildings and four others, organized by Washington Inner-City Self Help, a black organizing corps, established the Southern Columbia Heights Tenants Union (SCHTU). The coalition brought together people in a four-square-block area to deal with their problems.

The beginning point for all the work was relationship with our neighbors. Typical of our start in all the buildings, organizing began in one as a result of conversations with Joan, the neighborhood school crossing guard. She described to Jim the history of neglect that her building had suffered.

After several months of meetings and no response from the landlord to making basic repairs, tenants of twenty-four of the building's thirty-two inhabited apartments decided to pay their rent into an escrow account rather than to the owner. People who months before had hardly known one another, and certainly wouldn't have trusted one another with their money, were now putting their rent money—the largest single expense they had—into a common account.

The owner and his attorney were dumbfounded when those

who had been summonsed to court for eviction proceedings met with them in the lobby of the court, not as fearful individuals seeking mercy and a second chance, but as representatives of 67 percent of the tenants of the building, who were withholding their rent and prepared to fight him in court if necessary. The threat of court action, the very tool that owners used to intimidate individual tenants, was turned around and used by a unified group of people to cause the owner to back down.

He agreed to a month-by-month schedule of repairs with the understanding that the rent for each month would be held in escrow until that month's repairs were completed. The tenants celebrated their victory.

But months passed again, repairs were untouched, and the money continued to accumulate in the escrow account. Together, we began to think of the impossible. With $11,000 in the account, we looked toward raising enough money for the tenants association to buy the building, listed at $375,000—an idea which seemed foreign at best and most often crazy to tenants whose incomes barely stretched from the beginning of the month to the end. Their struggle simply to survive was brought home to Jim when one woman called at Christmas to ask if she could forego paying her rent into the account that month because she had to buy herself a pair of boots.

The immensity of the task was compounded by an appraisal that estimated it would cost $10,000 per unit to get the building up to decent standards. That added an additional cost, above purchase price, of almost half a million dollars.

After a year's accumulation of money from the rent strike, and successful negotiations that lowered the purchase price to $318,000, the tenants bought their building on May 23, 1981. They hoped for a federal Section VIII loan from HUD (Housing and Urban Development) to cover major rehabilitation and rent subsidies. They made their application to HUD, and it was being successfully processed through all the bureaucratic channels, giving great encouragement to the tenants association.

Then the changing of the guard in official Washington squelched the dream. Ronald Reagan moved the administration of Section VIII out of HUD and into a city agency. The tenants association had to fill out the three-inch-thick application all over again and submit it to the city. But the program was modified and cut back so drastically that all hope was erased.

The tenants still own their building, but it stands 50 percent vacant. They cannot afford to bring the empty apartments up to a livable level to attract more tenants. There is a good possibility that within a year they will not have the financial resources to continue running the building. Whether the dream can be kept alive is very much an open question.

Despite setbacks that official Washington deals us, our housing ministry continues to grow. We now have four community organizers in more than thirty buildings, each with its own active tenants association, as well as a staff member from the neighborhood. There have been a number of successful rent strikes, court victories, and demonstrations at city hall and even at landlords' homes.

We have won both small improvements and major victories. Locks have been put on doors, garbage picked up, heat turned on, hot water running again, building code violations corrected, evictions blocked, and even some legislative victories as tenants have filled the city council chambers at times of key votes.

Three other buildings have already either become, or are on their way to becoming, tenant-owned cooperatives. Three years ago people in our neighborhood couldn't even get a call through to the city's downtown offices when they were trying to find answers to their housing problems. Now, city council members show up at meetings of SCHTU.

Among our neighbors we are seeing a new era of solidarity, friendship, and cooperation. More than one hundred and fifty people attended SCHTU's last neighborhood tenant congress and spent a day talking about their common problems and struggles. We're discovering that hope can be as infectious as despair.

The organizing is an intense political struggle, but at the same time a very personal one. Jim Tamialis recently shared with us the truth he has found in words of Thomas Merton, from a personal letter Merton wrote to a friend: "A great deal has to be gone through, as gradually you struggle less and less for an idea and more and more for specific people. The range tends to narrow down, but it gets much more real."

The same truth has been discovered in our commitment to day-care for children in the neighborhood and the relationships with families it has brought us. Since the first days of the household pilot program we tried to provide a secure and nurturing environment in which children could grow in their relations to one another and the world around them, as well as cognitively prepare for a successful public school experience in this city which badly needs quality education.

In the fall of 1977, we opened up the Sojourners Daycare Center in the basement of Clifton Terrace Apartments, a low-income housing project owned by HUD, a few blocks from our households. The center provided low-cost day-care primarily for the children of our own community and of single parents from the neighborhood who worked at minimum wage or on-the-job training programs and were unable to afford the high cost of child care in D.C. The center eventually grew to include eight staff members, three neighborhood volunteers, and thirty-five children under the direction of Barb Tamialis.

In the spring of 1980, we reevaluated our work in the neighborhood and realized that we did not want to continue as maintainers of the center, but wanted to find a way to enable our neighbors to take a strong role in its development and future. We outlined our desire to transform the program into a neighborhood-run center and received the enthusiasm of parents who made comments like, "Three years ago there was nothing here. Now the children of this neighborhood have a day-care center so that parents can work and children can be prepared for school. Whatever we have to do to keep this center going, I'll help with it."

This parent, along with three others, four neighborhood leaders, and four members of Sojourners Fellowship, formed a board of directors to help the center in its transition toward neighborhood control. On October 1, 1980, the center was incorporated as a non-profit institution independent of Sojourners.

To signify the change, we decided the center should have a new name. Choosing it was quite a task. Those of us from Sojourners felt that it should reflect the neighborhood's commitment; but to the parents, "Sojourners" was its name, and they wanted to keep it. After several months of discussion, the board agreed on "Sojourner Truth Child Development Center," which retained the "Sojourner" but reflected the independence and pride of a great black woman whose legacy lives on in the neighborhood.

Enthusiasm carried us for a while as we struggled to make the transition. But the board we had called together never successfully took control, carried the vision, or found the time to do the necessary work in the midst of the members' busy lives.

Then, exactly a year after the day the center had been incorporated as an institution independent of us, the government again nailed the door shut on our efforts and hopes when the Reagan budget cuts took effect on October 1, 1981. Many parents lost their job-training funds as CETA (Comprehensive Education and Training Act) money dried up and jobs were abolished. Even those parents not supported by government programs began to feel the economic crunch, and many could no longer keep steady employment, which led to decreasing demand for child care and declining enrollment.

The tenants association of Clifton Terrace made a slide show of the center and presented it to HUD with a request for reduction of its rent so that the center could continue. The official response was that in a building owned by HUD we needed to be able to pay the fair market price in order to continue operating. One parent and board member said angrily, "The problem is, HUD doesn't see you as white folks.

They see you as being black, just like us, because of what you are doing. They don't want you here any more than they want us here!"

Unable to beat either the system or our own failings, we had to let the center die in February of 1982. One mother expressed her disappointment over having waited a year for her daughter to be old enough to enter the center only to find it closing. Others asked if we could hold our traditional graduation exercises before it closed, since we wouldn't be able to have them in August. It had always been very important to the parents that their children "graduate" from the center formally—maybe because most of them never had their own graduations. The graduation took place, the center shut its doors, and both neighborhood and community still grieve the loss.

I was sitting in a jail cell on October 1, 1981, the consequence of a peace protest, when the budget cuts took effect. It was an appropriate and instructive place to reflect on our nation's social priorities and the ironies and brutalities of the tale of two cities.

In the D.C. jail the talk is tough, but at night grown men cry. This well of human sadness is also a cavern of fear. Here are men who have lost control over their lives. Many are no more than eighteen or nineteen years old. They are at the mercy of a system that has never treated them well and now doesn't care about them at all. Parole officers and counselors forget about them, lawyers never come back, families and friends give up, and the guards have a standard reply to every request, "We'll see what we can do about it."

Everybody talks in jail but nobody listens. To listen, really listen, is a genuine pastoral ministry. I have seldom been in a situation that is more opportune for honest personal talk, true pastoral work, confession, prayer, and biblical reflection.

A forty-year-old man who has shot heroin since he was eighteen speaks of his children and weeps. Another asked a painful, probing question, "Can God forgive you if you've killed somebody?" Men wonder aloud if God hears the prayers of prisoners lying on their bunks at night. On the back wall of one cell a tangle of endless graffiti surrounds a beautiful penciled portrait of Jesus. Jesus is indeed among the prisoners, but you have to know how to look for him.

Most of the crimes for which the men have been jailed are ones done for money, or other crimes arising out of the problems of being poor. The very obvious fact in jail is that the vast majority of the men and women would not be there if they were not poor. That does not justify their crimes, but race and class are undeniably the most important factors in their incarceration.

Being white in the D.C. jail is an experience of extreme minority status. The form I filled out with vital statistics and fingerprints already had two lines filled in: Eyes—brown; Hair—black. Those had to be crossed out, and blue and brown substituted for me. The expectation is that this institution was built to lock up poor black people.

The action that put me behind bars was a protest outside the Sheraton Washington Hotel, where the Air Force Association was holding its annual nuclear weapons exposition. The theme of our protest was "Bread Not Bombs," linking the burgeoning defense budget with the cut-off of services needed for the survival of poor people.

Among my fellow prisoners I encountered strong support for our protest of nuclear weapons and the Reagan budget cuts. For all the lack of formal education, the level of political consciousness is remarkable. These men have a far more realistic view of how this country is run, why and for whom, than did the people with whom I went through years of higher education.

To make more and more bombs when there is not enough bread to go around seems particularly senseless and cruel from the vantage point of prisoners who are black and poor. They realize that their well-being has been sacrificed on the altars of national security.

7
At the Altars
of National Security

The Air Force Association's September weapons exposition, or "arms bazaar," is in some ways like a carnival, state fair, or auto show. But instead of magic shows, apple pies, or shiny new cars, this bazaar is a display of the most destructive weapons the world has ever seen.

More than thirty-five U.S. weapons manufacturers, such as Lockheed, General Electric, and Texas Instruments, bring their deadly wares to show them off to Pentagon officials, congresspeople, and agents of foreign governments. They seek to outdo one another, attempting to prove that their particular version of the MX or cruise missile is the most accurate and lethal, and provides "more bang for the buck." In the exhibition hall at the Sheraton Washington Hotel, displays, videotapes, and films show the aerospace industry's latest weapons in action.

For five years now, Sojourners has organized a Christian presence outside the hotel, keeping vigil as a counterwitness to the week-long carnival of death, and bearing testimony to the Prince of Peace. More than a thousand people come out to rally, sing, pray, leaflet, and take part in candlelight vigils.

Last year, on the evening of the bazaar's closing banquet, fifty-one of us stepped forward to offer bread to the makers of the bombs. When it was rejected, we knelt where we were in the hotel's main driveway. People in military dress uniforms and evening clothes who were on their way into the banquet had to pass through a gauntlet of candlelight, prayer, and song that three hundred friends had formed across the hotel entrance.

Those arriving in limousines and taxicabs had to wait for the bread carriers to be handcuffed, put in police wagons, and hauled away.

Our jail sentences were unusually stiff for a simple and peaceful sit-in. In the courtroom the judge stated his intention to discourage such protest. But official Washington's response has only strengthened our resolve to give a message to the people inside the hotel that their show is not welcome in our town. Efforts to shut down the arms bazaar have become a foundation of a growing grass-roots movement for peace in the Washington, D.C., area.

This year, for the first time in this city, black and white church leaders joined together in a united witness against the arms bazaar. The clear and public cooperation between black and white churches for the sake of peace and justice was a major breakthrough and a beginning of new possibilities for us here in Washington.

The Council of Churches of Greater Washington represents most of the Protestant churches, including the black churches which predominate in the city. This year, the council co-sponsored the arms bazaar protest with Sojourners. With the support also of the Catholic archdiocese, this year's witness for peace was almost unanimous in the churches in Washington, D.C.

On Sunday night, we began our week of witness with a "Peace and Justice Revival," held in front of the hotel. A large crowd of Christians joined for prayer, singing, Scripture reading, and forceful proclamation of the gospel. The unity of worship, witness, and action expressed that night and throughout the week was a powerful and deeply encouraging development for all of us. The Spirit has indeed been moving these days in Washington.

Increasing numbers of people everywhere are becoming concerned about nuclear war. Doctors tell us that there is no possible medical response to it. Lawyers say that nuclear war would be the greatest violation of international law in the history of the world.

Economists are beginning to realize that military spending is hurting the economy. Labor leaders have come to see that weapons-making provides fewer jobs than civilian work. Environmentalists fear the destruction of the ecological order. Families are worried about the future of their children.

Americans in larger and larger numbers believe that nuclear war is a threat to their survival. They question what would happen to their own cities in the event of a nuclear holocaust. What would it be like in Detroit, New York, San Francisco, following a nuclear war?

Arms control experts and scientists around the world are describing the prospect of nuclear war by the end of the century as "probable" and even "inevitable." The awful truth is that the superpowers are planning for nuclear war.

The nuclear powers continue to tell their own populations and the rest of the world the most insidious lie of our times—that these weapons of total destruction are necessary for self-defense, for deterrence, for keeping peace. Meanwhile, military planners and corporate profiteers push further and further beyond the threshold of nuclear overkill, relentlessly seeking a formula for winning.

For the first time, the human technology of war has the potential to destroy all that God has made. With our nuclear weapons, we have taken the power of life and death into our own hands. That is to say, we are guilty of seeking to take the place of God. Therefore the nuclear arms race is a blasphemy, a rebellion, a heresy, a sin against God. It is not only a sin against earth, but a sin against heaven itself. The production, possession, and threatened use of nuclear weapons is nothing less than the most arrogant human assault on the Creator and Redeemer of the world.

To prepare and plan for a nuclear war in which tens and hundreds of millions of people would die in the name of national security is to exalt our nation, our system, our principles, above everything else, even the survival of God's creation. The Bible calls that idolatry.

Our nation worships at the altar of national security. This

false and alien god has entered into the household of faith and corrupted the worship of Christians. To build weapons of ultimate destruction and to be ready to use them are the marks of a people who are in danger of losing not only their minds but their souls as well.

As a magazine and a community of faith, we at Sojourners have committed ourselves to putting the nuclear issue before the Christian community as the greatest test of our belief in the gospel in our time. We are investing our spiritual, physical, and journalistic resources in the struggle to stop our nation's present course of nuclear suicide. At the heart of our work is raising the issue of nuclear war in the churches.

Our witness has taken us to the Pentagon, Rocky Flats, and New York City. We have journeyed to Groton, Connecticut, to stand with friends in protest of the commissioning and launching of Trident submarines. We have done street theater on the steps of the Capitol. And every August finds us in candlelight procession at the White House in commemoration of the bombings of Hiroshima and Nagasaki.

For several years we encouraged churches to observe Memorial Day, not in the traditional way of honoring the war dead, but in a prayerful awareness of potential dead in a nuclear war. Churches all over the country have used the day as a time of worship and protest of nuclear policy.

Last year Pentecost fell on Memorial Day. We joined with several other groups who have sponsored "Peace Sabbath" to call for a "Weekend of Witness and Worship" around the theme of Deuteronomy 30:19: "Therefore choose life, that you and your descendants may live." More than ten thousand congregations held services, and many then made pilgrimages to local nuclear weapons facilities.

Recently a veteran political reporter said to me, "There is no question that a peace movement is emerging in opposition to nuclear weapons, and the foundation of it is in the churches." The ecumenical nature of the movement came home when members of our community found themselves at the large June 12 rally in New York during the UN Second Special

Session on Disarmament tucked between a Mennonite family and a Franciscan community. Friends from a Baptist church in Kansas City were not far behind.

Since the Reagan victory, the political Right has sought to consolidate its gains. Forces both inside and outside the government are moving to define a political consensus further to the right than ever before. Central to that consensus is the idea that most of the world's problems and conflicts are directly traceable to Moscow and its allies. Every development against U.S. interests is conveniently blamed on the Soviets.

Such is the argument for our U.S. intervention in many places around the globe. The vindictive rhetoric of opposition to communism has recently been nowhere so blatant as in Central America. The Reagan administration has chosen tiny El Salvador as the nation in which to place its ideological stakes and draw the line on communism.

The churches also lead a growing opposition to Reagan's ruthless policy in that country, the courageous testimony of sisters and brothers in the persecuted church of El Salvador carrying more weight with growing numbers of North American Christians than the pronouncements of the State Department. U.S. policies in El Salvador and throughout Central America are putting the U.S. government on a collision course with many of us in the churches.

The violence we are witnessing in El Salvador is a picture of the demonic. Amnesty International reports and documents the systematic repression of human rights, the torture and murder of thousands of innocent men, women, and children by the military security forces of El Salvador. The brutal rape and murder in 1980 of four religious women from the United States brought to public attention what has happened to tens of thousands of Salvadorans.

The real causes of the civil war in El Salvador are the grinding poverty of the majority of the people, the control of the country by an elite of wealthy landowners, and the reign of terror being carried out by the military to enforce the rule of the few over the many. The Reagan administration's refusal to acknowledge that injustice while blaming outside parties is both morally dishonest and politically foolish.

Its hostility toward Nicaragua has precipitated an arms buildup and state of emergency in that country. Now, the U.S. government is carrying out a CIA plan for covert paramilitary operations against Nicaragua, including the training of anti-Nicaraguan forces and the recruitment of a mercenary army to invade and carry out acts of terrorism in that country.

The only clear evidence of massive outside intervention in Central America is that of U.S. involvement. We have sent hundreds of millions of dollars in military aid to El Salvador and the surrounding dictatorial regimes, and we are responsible for the sophisticated weapons and heavy firepower that are turning the whole region into a war zone. Our military advisers are helping the Salvadoran military, and we have trained hundreds of Salvadoran officers and troops at bases in the United States.

The violence born of poverty and repression is only being made worse by outside interference and the insistence on military solutions. A just political settlement of the internal situation is the only means of averting more bloodshed. Our government is now making the same mistake in El Salvador that it made in Vietnam.

The two superpowers have shown themselves to be more alike than different in their approach to the rest of the world. We watched for many months with great hope the emergence of Solidarity in Poland. And then we saw hope dashed as the military took control, martial law was imposed, and Solidarity's leadership was arrested.

The pain of Poland's agony was only worsened by the self-righteous pronouncements of our own government. Reagan and then Secretary of State Haig indignantly assailed the Polish government and its Soviet supporters for suppressing unions, crushing freedom, flagrantly diregarding due process of law, and denying human rights: how dare the Soviets impose their will on another people through the brutality of a client regime that couldn't exist without their support?

The Soviet Union's client state in Warsaw is our military regime in San Salvador. The Soviets are responsible for crushed freedom in Poland, but we are responsible for murdered peasants and priests in El Salvador. The Soviets have blamed their Polish troubles on the American CIA, which makes about as much sense as U.S. charges of Soviet intervention in Central America. And they are mightily indignant about American imperialism while they preside over the destruction of freedom in Poland and Afghanistan. The words of the gospel speak directly to the situation: "How can you say to your brother, 'Let me take the speck out of your eye' when there is the log in your own eye?" (Matt. 7:4).

The people of El Salvador weep with the people of Poland, as do the poor of Guatemala, South Korea, the Philippines, Chile, Argentina, and every other place where military rule has been imposed, human rights trampled, people imprisoned, tortured, and killed all with the support of the United States government, first cousin to the Soviet Union.

We can expect the superpowers to slaughter the innocents then attack each other for doing so. The innocents cry out in Polish, Spanish, and every other language. The Herods never hear. But we do, and we must listen with our whole hearts.

Our community has listened carefully over the last few years to the church in El Salvador. The faithful and courageous witness of the church under persecution has been a continuing point of conversion for us. As the death toll of priests, catechists, and laypeople—and even an archbishop—mount, we have found ourselves in deep solidarity with their suffering.

El Salvador has been a tutor for the community as Vietnam once was. Younger members of the community used to ask me about Vietnam, requesting stories about the student movement and books about U.S. involvement to read. They don't ask anymore, because El Salvador has shown them the same truths that Vietnam revealed to me.

Joyce Hollyday in particular has become deeply involved, writing extensively about the political situation and the persecution of the church in El Salvador. I have seen in her the hurt, anger, passion, and determination that I first felt over Vietnam.

In a worship service commemorating the second anniversary of the assassination of Archbishop Oscar Romero, she preached and then joined Mernie King at the Eucharist table to serve the bread and wine. During the Eucharist, both preacher and celebrant were quietly weeping as they recognized the broken bodies and shed blood of the people of El Salvador in the body and blood of Christ.

A son of U.S. missionaries to Latin America, who had lived most of his life there and identified deeply with the people, was worshiping with us that night. He rose to share how important it was to him to see North Americans crying over the suffering of Latin Americans.

Every member of the community in their own way has wept over El Salvador. Many have kept vigil every Friday afternoon at the State Department with other concerned Christians in the city, a weekly vigil that has endured for more than two years.

Last year during Holy Week we walked with national church leaders through the streets of Washington, pausing for worship and prayer at chosen "stations of the cross." These were sites chosen for their complicity in the Passion that is now the daily life of the people of El Salvador—the White House, World Bank, Inter-American Defense Board, and State Department.

A few years before, during Lent, we kept vigil and set up torture tableaux at a broader range of sites as part of a human rights campaign. The campaign's purpose was to draw attention to the violation of human rights in countries from left to right along the political spectrum. We remembered and prayed for those forced into Soviet psychiatric hospitals in punishment for their opposition, as well as for those in the jails and torture chambers of Latin American military regimes.

While many Christians have learned to listen to the suffering, those in power seem even more entrenched in policies which are deaf to the cries of the poor. Apparently, many Americans still don't want to face the fact that our government has become a consistent supporter of dictatorship around the world. They still don't want to recognize what it means for the United States' best friends to be men like the shah of Iran, or Somoza of Nicaragua, Park of South Korea, Marcos of the Philippines, Pinochet of Chile, and a host of others.

We should have learned from the Iranian crisis that to support dictators who oppress their people is to ensure that our nation becomes a target of these people's hatred. That hate may take decades to develop into social revolution, but ultimately revolutions will come. To ignore that historical inevitability or to point only to the failures of revolutions is both a moral and political failure.

United States support for dictatorships around the world is sowing the seeds of violence that will grow to turn back on us. Already, the United States has become feared and hated in the poorer countries of the world because of our support for tyranny.

The Bible says if we sow the wind, we will reap the whirlwind. If we don't change our course, the Iranian crisis will be repeated in different forms and circumstances around the world.

However, the U.S. political climate is not very congenial to the spirit of reflection and repentance. Instead, the cry is to get tough and show the world that we can't be pushed around. The volatile responses of an insecure superpower sensing its loss of control in the world hold great potential for violence. If our national pride and arrogance prevail over our reason and compassion, we will indeed reap the whirlwind.

That cry to get tough has been fueled recently by the revival of draft registration. The nation wants to be prepared to mobilize its young men should they be needed for conflicts in various parts of the world. Since the use of nuclear weapons will most likely result from the escalation of a conventional war, any conflict involving the nuclear powers must be seen as increasing the chances of nuclear war.

At Sojourners we have determined to refuse the call to arms

at every point, including registration for the draft. Further, we advocate that others likewise refuse, and we feel a pastoral responsibility toward those who do.

A *Sojourners* reader from Minnesota sent me an article telling the story of a twenty-year-old draft resister. His picture was in the article, and I spotted something familiar. Under his arm, along with notebooks and papers, was a copy of *Sojourners*.

I thought that perhaps he had found some encouragement and support from *Sojourners* for his decision to refuse draft registration. I hoped so. I've talked to a number of the young men who now face legal prosecution for their decision not to register.

The government is putting great pressure on them now. Half a million young men haven't registered for the draft, and the government is worried.

Of course, the reasons for such mass refusal to register are many and mixed. But it does show that a lot of young men don't want to join the military. The government can't prosecute 500,000 people, so it will try to make an example of a few and hope to scare the rest into compliance.

Ironically, those most likely to be singled out are those who have been most honest and outspoken about their decision, who have written letters to the Selective Service System or who have made their choice public. In other words, those who are resisting for reasons of conscience are more likely to be the targets of government prosecution than those who hope to slip between the cracks.

But conscience has always been the great threat to illegitimate power. The political authorities cannot bear it when we say that what they are asking us to do is wrong. Inconvenient, disruptive of personal career plans, too dangerous—these are all reasons they can better understand and deal with. The idea that anything could have a higher authority in our lives than the government's authority infuriates and threatens political rulers.

The demand of draft registration is a hard burden to carry at age eighteen, nineteen, or twenty. These young men are faced with choices at a very young age that most adults have yet to make.

The choices they are making puts the challenge back on those of us who are older. We who are no longer vulnerable to the draft must be even more outspoken and sacrificial in our own resistance. The draft resisters deserve our unequivocal support, both personally and publicly. They must not remain in jeopardy alone.

In encouraging them to confront the war system and break the law, we must be willing to do the same. Whether it be sacrificing career goals, suffering financial loss, refusing to pay our war taxes, committing civil disobedience, or spending time in jail, the protests of us all must increase. As the government makes the young an easy target, the rest of us must make sure the government has more and other targets for persecution.

Sometimes we worry about how effective our protest will be. Who can say what the results of our actions will ultimately be? The traditional calculus of cause and effect is always inadequate in such circumstances. A divine calculus is at work in the way that faith changes history. If we believe the Bible, we will know that our obedience to God is always what makes the most difference.

The effect of faithfulness is often hidden, especially at first. Change does come, often slowly and imperceptibly, but in ways that endure. In the end, things done for reasons of faith will survive.

So, we must take courage as we follow our hearts. Taking risks for reasons of faith is not only the right thing to do with one's life, it is also the most exciting. God's faithfulness and grace will always be more known to us in the fire of struggle. And we may also discover some divine irony and even humor.

I received a phone call from my younger brother Bill the night of August 5. He and eight other members of the Detroit Peace Community were planning to do civil disobedience the next day, on the thirty-seventh anniversary of the bombing of Hiroshima. He wanted to tell me what they were planning and ask me to pray for them.

I had often called Bill on the eve of doing civil disobedience. It seems we are developing a family tradition.

For a year and a half the Detroit Peace Community has been holding witnesses at Bendix, a corporation which manufactures essential parts of nuclear warheads. For many months, Christians have been going to Bendix to pray, leaflet, talk to employees, and hold worship services. The August 6 witness was to be held at the corporation's headquarters in Southfield, Michigan. Fittingly, my brother would be arrested in his hometown. He and the eight others entered the Bendix property to pray for peace.

The condition of the jail they were put in after their arrest was quite bad. For days, Bill was without a bed, blanket, or prison clothes. He slept on a concrete floor, his tennis shoe for a pillow, in a crowded, one-room holding tank where fifteen men shared a single toilet. No hot food was served. Meals consisted of Sugar Pops for breakfast and bologna sandwiches for lunch and supper.

Constant noise, transition of prisoners, and boredom were the round-the-clock routine. There was nothing to read, and nothing with which to write. And no visitors, including family, were allowed, except clergy. Fortunately, a phone in the cell provided some contact with the outside for prisoners who waited in line to use it.

Bill works as the director of a day-care center run by the Church of the Messiah, an Episcopal parish and Christian community of which he and his wife, Tess, are members. On the day of his release, Tess had to be in school, so another member of the community, with her two little girls, came to pick up Bill.

Two-year-old Lauren, a favorite of Bill's, gave him a big hug and a kiss. Then she peered around behind him as if looking for someone. "Where is God?" she asked. Bill looked puzzled.

Lauren's mother, Becky, described the conversation she had just had with her two daughters on the way to the jail.

"Do you know where we are going?" she asked them.

"Yes," they replied, "to jail."

"Why are we going to jail?" she asked.

"To get Bill out of jail and to get God out of jail."

The mother asked, "What do you mean, get God out of jail?" Her little girl said, "All week long we've been praying that God would be with Bill in jail."

Non-payment of war taxes has also been a vital concern for Sojourners. When we put out the first issue of the magazine at the height of the Vietnam War, it became very clear that refusal of war tax payment was for us as morally necessary as our refusal of military induction. We could not oppose war in every other way and then help pay for it. We also refused then, and continue to refuse, payment of our telephone tax, which was instituted to help pay for the war.

The payment of taxes is the most basic, and from the government's point of view, most important way that we support the policies of the state. With hardly an afterthought, American Christians in recent times have given more money to underwrite military destruction and help build the most massive arsenal in human history than we have given to pay for relief, service, evangelism, missions, social action, and all the programs of the churches combined.

The state's demand for war taxes puts many Christians in a dilemma in which peace claims their commitment but war claims their money. Personal and corporate response to the payment of war taxes is a thorny and serious question, one which must become a matter of much more public discussion and discernment in the Christian community.

With the heightening nuclear arms race and the widening conflict in Central America, our stand on war tax resistance has remained resolute: we cannot with good conscience provide our government, through our tax dollars, with the necessary means for its nuclear threats and ideological military exploits.

Our war tax resistance is both institutional and personal. A non-profit corporation provides a legal entity for our magazine, as well as our peace and neighborhood ministries. Everyone working in these ministries earns a subsistence income. For most of us, subsistence is below the taxable level.

For others, a small tax liability is incurred. Like all organizations, we are legally bound to withhold federal income taxes (including war taxes) from the salaries of liable employees and to submit them to the government. Since we refuse to serve as a war-tax gathering agency, we decided years ago not to submit federal income taxes from these employees' wages. To date, the Internal Revenue Service has threatened to retaliate, including taking us to court. So far, it has settled for levying our bank account.

Joe Roos and I were once called down to the IRS office to account for the magazine's refusal to withhold taxes from our employees. This was our first interview, at the lowest rung of the IRS ladder.

A young IRS worker was conducting the interview. He said he wanted to take the case to his supervisor and would soon return.

He came back a short while later, smiled, and said, "Well, you don't have to pay." Joe and I looked at each other rather incredulously, and I said to the young man, "Either you don't quite understand what we're doing, or the three of us have just made tax history."

He had mistakenly thought that we were seeking exemption from Social Security payments, which as a non-profit corporation we are not required to pay. I explained to him that it was our taxes that we weren't paying.

"Oh," he said, "I think I'd better go back and see my supervisor."

He returned again after a while, smiling, and said, "Well, it's just as I thought. You *do* have to pay."

Joe and I grinned at each other, and I said, "Well, you see, we know that we are legally required to withhold and send in all this tax. But our Christian convictions won't allow us to do that. So I think we have a conflict here."

At first he seemed not to understand. But then the light of recognition came over his face. "Oh, I get it," he said. "Kind of like what Muhammed Ali did."

"Well, kind of," I replied.

He looked around to make sure no one else was listening before he leaned forward, clasped my hand, and said in a whisper, "Right on, man. Fight it all the way to the top."

We are equally committed to war-tax resistance as individuals. All members of Sojourners Fellowship pool our incomes. Nearly two-thirds of the community earn below the taxable income level, have no personal income, or are children. None of these incur any war-tax liability.

The rest of the community earns taxable incomes. Where that income is not subject to employer withholding, we have refused payment of war taxes. Some have had less tax withheld than was due and refused to pay the remainder. Those whose taxes are automatically withheld have employed various methods of reducing their war-tax liability to zero, sometimes with limited success. Our commitment is that no member of Sojourners Fellowship pays war taxes.

When you refuse to pay a portion of your income tax, you begin to get a series of letters from the IRS. At first they are very polite: "Oh, so you forgot to pay all of your taxes. Well, that's okay, just send your check in as soon as possible."

A few weeks go by and you get another letter a little more serious and demanding: "You did not fulfill all your tax liability. Send it to the IRS immediately."

The next letter becomes rather hostile: "Our records show that you have not paid all the taxes due to us. If you do not pay immediately, you will be legally prosecuted."

Eventually, the letters become downright threatening: "We have sought a lien on all of your property in the District of Columbia. If you do not remit immediately, your property will be confiscated."

Each year I have dutifully responded to each of these letters. I wrote back and always enclosed a photocopy of the original letter I sent in with my tax return before April 15, explaining why, for reasons of Christian conscience, I could not pay that portion of my taxes that went to support the military. But no matter what I did, I always got the same succession of letters.

Finally, one day I realized there was no one on the other end of my correspondence—only a computer with programmed responses designed to get more nasty every week the tax money didn't come in. So I've come up with an idea.

We recently purchased a small computer at *Sojourners* to maintain our subscription list and print address labels. What if we could program into our computer responses, escalating peacefully, to answer the letters from the IRS? That way the computers could just fight it out.

The IRS finally decided to pay me a visit in person and audit me as a result of my continual war-tax refusal. I could tell that the IRS agent was nervous by the way he was chain-smoking. At the end of our conversation, he admitted to me that he had been told by the IRS that he was going to be auditing some "radicals" and was warned to "be careful" because "they probably have guns."

The first thing he said, with fear and agitation, was, "Now, I don't want to talk about politics. I'm just here to do an audit." Joe was there with the records of both my personal and our community finances. We assured the IRS agent that we bore no hostility toward him and wanted simply to be helpful in giving him the information he needed. He seemed to relax a little after that.

He asked to see the records of my checking account. I told him I didn't have one, and that all of my personal financial records were in the large community ledger Joe had brought to the meeting and placed on the desk before him. Joe patiently explained our system of economic sharing and bookkeeping. The agent seemed mystified.

"But don't you get any money for yourself?" he asked.

"Yes," I explained. "Beyond all of our living expenses that are corporately met, each member of the community gets fifteen dollars a month for personal spending."

"You're kidding," he said.

"No," I replied. And he dropped his pencil on the floor.

"But you're the editor here, right?"

I nodded.

"And you make the same salary as everyone else?"

"Well, actually, no," I answered.

"I thought so," he replied.

"The shipping clerk makes more than I do because he is not a member of the community and has higher personal expenses than I do."

He looked completely incredulous as he said, "In all my years working for the IRS, I have never run into anything like this. Do you realize that there is absolutely no economic incentive in your life?"

He went on to ask, "Why do you people live this way?" There was my opening. I began to speak about the gospel, the way of Jesus, and the economic sharing of the early church. We were just trying to make those things real in our own experience, I told him.

A glimmer of understanding came into his eyes, and he said with a smile, "Oh, I bet I can guess then why you aren't paying all your taxes."

"You're catching on," I said, and then explained how I had decided not to pay taxes for war because of my Christian convictions.

"Well, can I ask you a question?" he responded. "What about the Russians? If we laid down our arms, wouldn't they take us over?"

"That's a good question," I replied. "Let's talk about it." For a man who didn't want to talk about politics, he got deeply involved in our conversation about war, peace, and the gospel.

When it was over, he said, "You know, this really makes a lot of sense to me. Now, I'm not ready to refuse to pay my own taxes, you understand, but. . . ." there he was, an agent for the IRS, in a serious conversation about whether he should continue to pay his own taxes for war. It felt like quite an evangelistic conversation to me. Before he left, he told us that we were the nicest people he ever had to audit and wished me luck.

Christian payment of war taxes often goes on without question because the connection between the turning over of our money and the suffering of the victims of our military policies seems obscure. The victims of current wars and potential victims in a nuclear war remain for the most part invisible to us.

As I write this chapter, the commemoration of the atomic bombings of Hiroshima and Nagasaki are upon us. Last night we gathered again across from the White House with candles. We gathered not to proclaim a cause, but to remember a people.

Those of our community who were in New York for the huge peace rally last June 12 recall the members of a Japanese delegation, some from Hiroshima and Nagasaki, showering the crowd with chains of paper cranes, colorful, intricate, peace offerings. A people our country deeply wronged, they remind us of the power of forgiveness.

For thirty-eight years the Japanese have tried to get us to see their pained faces since the atomic bombings. But we have been afraid of what we might see: agony, shock, horror. To look is to have to face up to what we have done. To look is to see our future and our children's future written on their faces.

The devastation and horror we wreaked on Hiroshima and its sister city of Nagasaki are beyond imagination. The agony lives on in those who lost family members in the bombings, continue to lose them to cancer and radiation sickness, and discover the legacy of the bombings in generations of children who suffer genetic defects.

We have the capacity now to create more than one million Hiroshimas, and every day we add three more bombs to our arsenal. We have come this far by not looking at the faces of the people of Hiroshima and by not looking at the faces of those we now call our enemies.

An Israeli soldier in Lebanon said of the peole he was ordered to kill, "It's so hard when I'm up close. When I can see their faces, I can't bring myself to kill them. But when I'm farther away and am just shooting artillery shells, then I can do it."

A young American in a missile silo, one of many with his finger on the nuclear button, said, "I don't know if I could kill anyone up close. This way I never have to see who my missile hits."

Our missiles are aimed at the Soviet threat, the Russian system, godless communism. But our missiles will hit people, families, children. Hundreds of millions of them. Just like in Hiroshima and Nagasaki. They will hit churches and kill millions of sisters and brothers who are one with us in the body of Christ.

It is a great historical irony that there were Catholics in the bombing crew that dropped the bomb on Nagasaki, the first and largest Catholic city in Japan. The ground zero target for the bomb was the Catholic cathedral. Among its victims were hundreds of worshipers and three orders of Catholic sisters.

The faces of Hiroshima and Nagasaki look at us quietly, patiently, earnestly, to show us the human face of nuclear war. They refuse to turn away from our eyes as we have turned away from theirs. They say, "See what you have done. See what is the fate of the earth unless you stop the mad race of nuclear weapons."

In the name of national security or any other name, we can no longer turn away from our own flesh. We went to the White House again to say to the nation's leaders, "In the name of God, look at the faces."

The words of Paul speak right to the heart of our problem: "But now in Christ Jesus you who once were far off have been brought near in the blood of Christ. For he is our peace, who has made us both one, and has broken down the dividing wall of hostility, by abolishing in his flesh the law of commandments and ordinances, that he might create in himself one new [humanity] in place of the two, so making peace, and might reconcile us to God in one body through the cross, thereby bringing the hostility to an end" (Eph. 2:13-16).

At the time that these words were written, it was the Jews and Gentiles who were "far off." But today, when we think of who is farthest away from American Christians, we think of the Russians. They are the most feared, caricatured, unknown, inhuman to us. But the Russians have been brought near to us by the blood of Christ.

There is no peace through strength, through balance of

terror, through military superiority; there is peace only through the cross. The hostility which God has put to death our government would stir up, and in so doing has directly set itself and our nation against the work of the cross of Jesus Christ.

The arms race will not end until we come to terms with the Russians. The nuclear freeze won't be enough; arms control won't be enough. Mutual fear and distrust will destroy us unless we overcome it. And the way to overcome it is the way of the cross.

The Bible makes clear the mission of the church. We must step out, walk around diplomatic channels, ignore the obstacles, break the laws, and make friends of our enemies—American churches to Russian churches, American families to Russian families. We must build the bonds strong enough to defend both sides from nuclear weapons. And in so doing, we could make the words of Paul a prophecy for our future.

Paul tells us in another of his letters that we are to "regard no one from a human point of view" (II Cor. 5:16). That means that we can no longer look at one another as Russians, Americans, communists, capitalists, guerrillas, enemies, or aliens—but as sisters and brothers, children of the same God.

But first we must allow ourselves to look closely. Official Washington would isolate us from our enemies across the globe and from the poor in our own cities. But we have been given the eyes of Christ to see himself in their faces. It is Christ whom we assault in our inner cities. It is Christ who was recrucified at Hiroshima, and who will be the ultimate victim in the next nuclear war.

We must see now before it is too late. Unless we see a neighbor in the face of the enemy now, we will have no future worth speaking of. But if we look, really look, at the face of our enemy, we might end our warring madness, heal our terrible wounds, and renew the face of the earth.

8
Idols Closer to Home

Sojourners has written much and often about the abuse and cheapening of grace. In many ways, it is the place where we began. That concern still stands; cheap grace continues to be the greatest affliction of the churches.

Those who pursue radical discipleship, however, face another problem. It is the tendency to seek justification in our life-style, our work, our protest, our causes, our movements, our actions, our prophetic identity, and our radical self-image. It becomes an easy temptation to place our security in the things we stand for and in the things we do, instead of in what God has done. It is a temptation to depend on things other than God's grace.

"For by grace you have been saved through faith; and this is not your own doing, it is the gift of God—not because of works, lest [anyone] should boast." (Eph. 2:8-9). Grace is the logic of a loving God. There is nothing we can do to earn it, win it, or deserve it. Grace is simply a gift, not a reward. We can receive it only by faith, not through good works.

As familiar as that is to us, we have great difficulty coming to terms with the meaning and reality of grace. We seem to find innumerable ways to deny the grace that is the free gift of God's love to us. Either we abuse it and make grace self-serving, or we dismiss its reality altogether by acting to establish our own righteousness. In twisting God's purposes to suit our own or in striving to justify ourselves through our own efforts, we have, in fact, denied the grace of God. In so doing, we have denied ourselves the ability to simply rest in that grace, to be changed and used by God's love.

Perhaps the greatest denial of grace in our time lies in its abuse. Dietrich Bonhoeffer named it "cheap grace." The grace of God is cheapened and distorted when used to cover over our sin rather than to cleanse it. The language of grace is impoverished and exploited when employed to justify our disobedience and lukewarmness.

True grace convicts of sin, softens the heart, and prompts repentance. Cheap grace overlooks sin, hardens the heart, and breeds complacency. True grace accepts and redeems the sinner. Cheap grace accommodates to and justifies the sin.

As Bonhoeffer reminds us, grace which comes at such a heavy cost to God cannot be used cheaply. Grace is not meant to obscure the path of discipleship and obedience. On the contrary, grace opens that path to us. Cheap grace proclaims salvation without repentance. The evangelism of cheap grace has no real power to challenge either our personal status or the political status quo.

But there is another denial of grace among us. It often rears up in reaction to the cheap grace most prevalent in our churches.

The reaction to cheap grace can be so strong, the emphasis on radical discipleship and obedience so firm, that eventually there is little room left for *any* grace in our lives. The response to cheap grace can wrongly lead us to the loss of grace altogether. In our reaction against cheap grace, we are always in danger of producing radical alternatives to grace, new forms of works righteousness. In our desire to be obedient to the gospel and to prove our faithfulness, we could lose the freedom and the power that come from resting and fully trusting in God's grace as sufficient for our lives and for the world.

In the language of the Ephesians passage, radical Christians have things they tend to "boast of." These are the things that can most easily become idols for us. They are not the idolatries of the established society and the comfortable church. We have identified those and confronted them so often that they have become familiar and easily recognizable. Therefore, their power over us has become diminished.

But there are idols closer to home. We are less able to recognize them and can, therefore, more easily fall into their grasp. In very subtle ways, they are the idolatries that have the most power over us.

Idolatry must be identified and unmasked if it is to lose its power. Illusion is, in fact, the source of an idol's power. We place our trust in that which is not trustworthy but appears to be. We are deceived by the image of the idol which replaces that which is worthy of our trust.

Not to fully trust God's grace is to engage in illusion. It is to underestimate the power of sin and death and to overestimate our ability to overcome it. Not to rely on the work of Christ is to rely on our own work to save ourselves and the world. When we don't trust grace, we take ourselves too seriously, while not taking sin seriously enough.

What are those things in which we are tempted to place a false trust, things that threaten to become idols for us, things that can become substitutes for grace?

To live simply is a biblical virtue, especially in a society choking on its own consumption and waste. Economic simplicity clears away the material obstacles that block dependence on God. Living with less also helps open our eyes to the suffering of the poor. It enables us to participate more easily in their struggle for justice, instead of in their oppression. The motive for living simply is that we might love both God and the poor more freely.

But it is not a simple life-style that justifies us. It is, rather, God's grace that enables us to live more simply. Displaying our style of life as if it were a badge of righteousness contradicts the whole spiritual foundation of economic simplicity. We live simply not out of obligation and guilt but to be less hindered in serving God and the poor. It should not be a duty, but a joy. Our life-style must not be used to judge others, but to invite them to share in the freedom and grace we have found.

It was the worst tendency of the Pharisees to seek justification before God through their scrupulous life-style. May we never be like the Pharisee (read: the wealthy corporation executive) who stood beside the tax collector and thanked God that he wasn't such a sinner. Complex legalisms employed in the name of simple living could well rob us of the freedom and joy which are the intended fruits of such a life-style.

That the God of the Bible is on the side of the poor and the oppressed is beyond dispute. Christ's presence among the lowly and the afflicted is a truth drawn from the very heart of the Gospels. But taking up the cause of the poor can have its own pitfalls.

There is a tendency among concerned people to romanticize the poor and their poverty. Poverty is ugly and bitter, and the poor suffer from the same sinful human condition as the rest of us. It is insensitive to represent them, and the brutal circumstances of their lives, as uniquely noble and virtuous. That may serve the fantasies of people experiencing downward mobility, but it will not serve the needs of poor people.

The suffering of the exploited is too easily exploitable. The misery of the poor advertises well to serve the personal, ideological, religious, and financial interests of others, and new forms of colonial exploitation replace old ones. The poor become the objects of public rhetoric, the targets of charity projects, and the pawns of political ambition. To use the poor for the sake of Christian ministry or leftist ideology is again to make capital out of their suffering. We have seen too much of religious and political radicals building their personal careers on the oppression of the poor.

Poor people are best served by those who desire to be their friends. We identify with the poor, not to save ourselves, but so that we might better identify with Christ. He is already among the suffering and forgotten ones and invites us to join him there. He has taught us to love and serve him by sharing his special passion for those who are loved the least.

The Scriptures tell us that love and truth show themselves in action and not merely in words. Direct action in the public arena has become a central means for bearing faithful witness, for making peace, and for seeking social justice. Those actions bring to light what is dangerous and wrong and point to a better way.

However, there is an inherent danger in public protest. Critical tests of any public action or campaign are: What or who is being made known and visible? Is the truth being made more clear? Or is a person, a group, an institution, or a movement being made more prominent?

All our public actions must be rooted in the power of love and truth. We act for the purpose of making that power known, not for the purpose of making ourselves known. Our motivation must be to open people's eyes to the truth, not to show ourselves as right and them as wrong.

Whenever our protest becomes an effort to "prove ourselves," we are in serious danger. Our best actions are those which admit our complicity in the evil we protest and are marked by a spirit of genuine repentance and humility. Our worst actions are those which seek to demonstrate our own righteousness, our purity, our freedom from complicity. When our pride overtakes our protest, we may simply be repeating, in political form, the self-righteous judgment of the fundamentalists—"I'm saved, and you're not."

One veteran Christian activist wrote: "I have seen so much of the 'heresy of good works' in the religious Left, a belief that is based on the arrogance that *we* have to save the world, and a very real denial (if not in words, then in actions) that the world has *already* been saved. And believe me, it is very tiresome to go around feeling like the fate of the world rests on your words and on your deeds. . . . Sometimes I think that numbers of arrests have replaced indulgences in the 'new church,' and that is *not* spiritual progress."

Our actions do not have the power to save us. Instead, they *can* have the power to make the truth known. Although the actions we undertake will never substitute for grace, they can indeed be witnesses of God's grace. Since they lack the capacity to justify us, a better purpose for our actions would be to bear faithful witness.

Because communication is so basic to public action, the nature of what we say and do becomes very important. Actions which mostly communicate a threatening and desperate spirit should be carefully questioned. Free and open evaluation of all public action is necessary to protect the health and character of our protest. The quality and integrity of what we communicate will be its most crucial element.

Action done in public will always carry with it the great danger of presumption. We ought to act with the awareness of how risky it is to claim to be making the truth known. The ever-present threat is to identify the truth with ourselves, instead of the other way around. Because of the inherent presumption of public protest, it should always reflect a spirit of confession, humility, and invitation.

Judgment, arrogance, and exclusiveness are signs of spiritual immaturity. Protest characterized by such things will have the effect of hardening hearts, confirming people's fears, and convincing them of their present opinions. Public action has sometimes done more harm than good. It can drive people away from the very things we are trying to say. It can perpetuate, as easily as dispel, public blindness.

Never has the absolute need for nonviolence been greater than in a world living under the nuclear shadow. But even our position on nonviolence can be self-serving and hide deeper motives.

Nonviolence aims for truth and not for power. Its chief weapon is the application of spiritual force, not the use of coercion. A very serious problem in nonviolent movements is the hidden aggression, the manipulation, the assertive ego, and the desire for provocation that can lurk beneath the surface of repetitive platitudes about the commitment to nonviolence. The rhetorical cloak of nonviolence can be used to hide the will to power that is the very foundation of violence. The desire to win over others, to defeat one's enemies, and to humiliate the opposition are all characteristics of violence and are too painfully evident in much of what is called nonviolent action.

The infighting, media grabbing, and intense competition of the peace movement are hardly evidence that the will to power has been overcome. Some of the worst tyrannies have been hidden behind anarchist principles and the myth of leaderless groups and communities.

We should know by now that all violence is of a piece. If that is true, then the violence of dissent is directly linked to the violence of the established order. It is, in fact, a mirror reflection of it. Therefore, the violence present in the peace movement can be said to be part of the violence that fuels the nuclear arms race. We can no longer justify the "excesses" of the peace movement by appealing to the greater violence of the system. The urgency of the nuclear situation calls for more, not less, care in the actions we undertake.

Nonviolence does not try to overcome the adversary by defeating him, but by convincing him. It turns an adversary into a friend, not by winning over her, but by winning her over. Knowing that today's enemy may become tomorrow's friend should cause us to examine our treatment of opponents more closely. It is interesting how people from the military and the defense industry who "defect" to the peace movement are transformed from demons into saints overnight.

Patience is central to nonviolence. Nonviolence is based on the kind of love the Bible speaks of as "enduring all things." Thomas Merton taught us that the root of war is fear. If that is true, we must become much more understanding of the fears people have. The most effective peacemakers are those who have experienced the healing of their own fears and can now help lead others out of theirs. There is still too much fear in the peace movement to heal the fears of a nation. How can we be peacemakers when we are still afraid of one another? Our hope is in deepening our experience of the "perfect love that casts out fear."

The prophetic vocation is deeply biblical and highly

dangerous. It is a calling most necessary for our time, but one which requires the most intense scrutiny.

Prophets have always challenged idolatry. The people of God forget who they are and to whom they belong. Before long, their forgetfulness causes them to fall into the false worship of idols. Prophets are then raised up to name the idolatries, to speak the word of the Lord, to lead the people out of their false worship, and to bring them back to God.

The need in our day is for clear words of God's judgment and mercy. The prophetic vocation is to faithfully communicate that judgment and mercy in a way people can hear and understand. A genuinely prophetic message will never show selectivity, partiality, or parochial interest. A prophet in the biblical tradition will not challenge some idols and leave others untouched. He or she will not rage against injustice and violence in some places and be strangely silent about oppression elsewhere.

It is painfully apparent that radical Christians have not always been true to the whole counsel of God's judgment. An ideological selectivity intrudes, a political bias which undermines the credibility and power of prophetic witness. The idolatries of the establishment are attacked while the idols of the anti-establishment receive less critical treatment. The evils of the majority culture are assailed but the sins of the counterculture are often passed over. The political prisoners of right-wing dictatorships seem to generate more interest than those languishing in the jails of the leftist regimes.

A long-time Christian pacifist recently wrote to me on this subject:

> A child dead from a revolutionary rocket we tend to see quite differently from one dead from an imperialist rocket. The revolutionary sponsors are guarded by the sanctuary of holy words that make certain allowances for dead children. The death is a tragedy rather than a crime against humanity. Actually, the other side is finally to blame for it. And so forth.
>
> Someone tortured in Chile, we find, is far more needful of response and protest than someone tortured in the Soviet

Union. A priest arrested in Argentina is a more pressing matter than a monk arrested in Vietnam. Indeed, the latter need hardly be noticed. The heavy-handed methods of the shah of Iran are a different kettle of fish than those of the Chinese or the Cubans. For the latter are merely breaking eggs in order to make an omelet, as it has often been put to me.

Political orthodoxy is anathema to prophetic integrity. The maintenance of the party line describes propaganda, not prophecy. Prophecy is, in fact, profoundly anti-ideological. Karl Barth once wrote:

> The Christian Church must be guided by the Word of God and by it alone. It must not forget for an instant that all political systems, right and left alike, are the work of men. It must hold itself free to carry out its own mission and to work out a possibly quite new form of obedience or resistance. It must not sell this birthright for any conservative or revolutionary mess of pottage.

Politicized theology is no substitute for prophetic witness. Radical proof-texting is no better than fundamentalist proof-texting. We are keenly aware of the conservative, militaristic, patriotic, racist, and sexist distortions of the Bible. Likewise, there can be neither a leftist agenda in reading the Scriptures, nor anarchist, nor pacifist, nor communitarian, nor any other bias, for that matter. The Word of God is intended to judge all our priorities, to overturn all our biases, to correct all our perceptions.

If the prophetic vocation is to bring the judgment of God to bear, then the prophet must be the first to be placed under that judgment. The prophetic calling must be, by definition, an extremely troubling one. It must be as troubling to ourselves as it is to those who bear the brunt of our prophetic pronouncements—or more so.

Smugness and complacency are the prophet's worst enemies. The hardest words of judgment must always be reserved for our own group. God's Word must be allowed to confront the idolatries closest to us before it will destroy those farthest away. Pride, alienation, and bitterness are the worst sources of prophetic zeal and will corrupt and distort our witness.

The biblical prophets loved the people, were a part of the people, and claimed them as their own. Therefore the disobedience and sin of the people hurt the prophets, and their first response to the people's faithlessness was grief, not indignation. The prophets were those who spoke the hard words. But they spoke with broken hearts.

The prophets would not conform to the people, but they never lost their relationship to them. Jesus, in the tradition of the prophets, showed just such a capacity to love the people without conforming to their sinful ways. In our desire not to be conformed to the sins of the nation, we could lose the capacity to identify with the people that is so basic to the prophetic calling.

Those who would avow a prophetic vocation to the church must ask themselves some questions: Do I love the church? Or do I hate it? God will not entrust us with a prophetic ministry merely to cloak our own rage and judgment. But if we love the church, if we love the people, if our hearts ache when we see their folly, then God may trust us to be vehicles of divine rage and judgment, to express God's purposes.

The most basic question for the prophet is to whom he or she is accountable. Prophets not accountable to anyone but themselves are a dangerous and destructive lot. Some of the worst things in history have been done out of prophetic zeal.

Grace saves the prophetic vocation. The knowledge and experience of grace can ease the seriousness with which we tend to take ourselves. Grace can restore our humility, our sense of humor, and our ability to laugh at ourselves. All are regularly needed by prophets. Only sinners make good prophets.

Radical Christians, like all creatures, tend to boast most of all of themselves. To trust in our life-style, our commitment to the poor, our actions, our nonviolence, or our prophetic identity is, in the end, to trust in ourselves. It is to trust in our work, our principles, our causes, and our self-images.

Idolatry is the worship of anything other than God. And an idol is simply an image. When we worship an idol, we are worshiping an image. How important our images are to us! Our lives can so easily become exercises in image-building.

We eschew success in the world, then pursue it through "alternative" channels. We snicker at the system's professionals while establishing a career in the movement. We leave worldly fame behind but enjoy the special status this society grants to its radicals and prophets. We rail against the power structure and build a power base of our own.

As the Bible says, "None is righteous, no, not one" (Rom. 3:10). Grace can overcome our greatest temptation: to believe that we are better than those who need convincing and converting. Grace imparts to us the capacity to forgive because we know that we have been forgiven. The marks of grace are gentleness, hope, and faith. The most dependable sign of its presence is joy.

To trust grace is to know that the world has already been saved by Jesus Christ. It is to know that we cannot save the world any more than we can save ourselves. All our work is done only in response to Christ's work. To receive the gift of grace is to let go of self-sufficiency and to act out of a spirit of gratitude.

Christians must pursue more than a successful strategy; we must seek a deeper faith. Only then will we have the assurance of salvation, not because of what we have accomplished, but because we have allowed God's grace and mercy to flow through our lives. We can be grateful that there are always a few among us who have given over their lives to be those very vessels of divine grace.

9
Two Teachers

The number of people touched by Dorothy Day is beyond counting. This evangelical boy from the Midwest was one.

I grew up being taught that the Bible should be taken literally. Dorothy Day is one of the few people I've ever met who actually did. She took the gospel at face value and based her life on it.

Dorothy did what Jesus said to do. She was the most thoroughly evangelical Christian of our time, though the movement by that name never claimed her as its own.

It was in the Depression year of 1933 that she and Peter Maurin founded *The Catholic Worker*. They sold the first copies of the newspaper on May Day for a penny each. "Read *The Daily Worker*," shouted the communists selling their paper to the unemployed in Washington Square. "Read *The Catholic Worker* daily," answered back a little band of Catholics who said their faith had made them radicals.

For half a century their paper has been the voice of a movement that has always concentrated on the basics of the gospel. Dorothy's grasp of her times was profound, but it was the simple things that captured her imagination and commitment—like the gospel being good news to the poor and the children of God living as peacemakers.

She always spoke of the "works of mercy" as the center of it all: feeding the hungry, housing the homeless, clothing the naked, comforting the lonely, sick, and imprisoned. For the cause of Christ, she literally spent her life on the side of the suffering and the afflicted, while relentlessly attacking the institutions and systems which lead to oppression and war.

In so doing she became an institution herself, and the Catholic Worker movement has served for fifty years as the heart and conscience of the American Catholic church and, for that matter, of American Christianity. Dorothy helped to found more than forty houses of hospitality and a dozen farms which became rare places that the poor could call home.

The poorest of the poor were Dorothy's constituency. Shunned by everyone else, they knew they could trust this woman. Streams of poor people from her Bowery neighborhood showed up at her funeral, mingling with the famous and powerful, but knowing that Dorothy belonged to them.

The voluntary poverty, service to the poor, and radical pacifism of the Catholic Worker kept the movement small, but influenced many over the years. For most of the volunteers, life at the Catholic Worker became a kind of school, an intense training ground in compassion that would shape the rest of their lives.

Like any radicalism that endures, Dorothy's was rooted in very traditional soil. Her unswerving loyalty to the teachings and traditions of the church often caused consternation among her more progressive friends. But it was the strength of that very commitment to the gospel that made Dorothy such a radical. And it was this radical traditionalism that proved troublesome to the church she loved.

That same combination of conservative religion and radical politics is the energy behind Sojourners and has become a point of strong solidarity between ourselves and the Catholic Worker movement. Probably the nicest thing anyone ever said about us was when some of our Catholic Worker friends in New York called Sojourners a "Protestant Catholic Worker."

Time spent with Dorothy Day was for me a deep reminder of the simple things. It was a confirmation of the fact that love and compassion are the strongest things, the truest things, the most powerful things, the most revolutionary things.

The testimony of Dorothy reminds me that the Christian life begins with love, that it also ends with love, that there is nothing we can do as Christians, nothing that we must become, that is prior to love. As we come to faith, we begin to love.

Sharing with those who cook the soup, make the beds, clean the floors, and care for the people at St. Joseph House and Maryhouse in New York brought to mind the words of the apostles. They suggested that love is the activity of faith, and that one who does not love does not know God.

In scripture, love has nothing to do with mere feeling, sentiment, or opinion. On the contrary, it consists of relationship and action. It is shaped by the quality of God's love for us. Dorothy seemed to understand that love is merely a reflection, a response to the way we are loved by Christ. To forget that is to fall victim to some idea of love in general, to some human emotion, and thus to derive our definition of Christian love from a false source.

The mark of God's love in us is the humility that comes of being crushed by the world's great need of love. The fact that we are overwhelmed by that continual claim upon our lives is a sign that the love of God is present within and among us.

To love, then, means to become what we already are—those who are loved by God. To love means a daily choice to live the life of faith and obedience. To love is to accept and confirm our calling, our vocation, our identity as God's people.

Much has been said about Dorothy Day and much more will be said. But perhaps the most important thing I can say is that she showed me what it means to be a Christian. She was a follower of Jesus Christ who fell in love with his kingdom and made it come alive in the most wretched circumstances of men and women. Dorothy believed that, in the end, "love is the measure." The following postscript is from her autobiography, *The Long Loneliness:*

> We were just sitting there talking when Peter Maurin came in.
> We were just sitting there talking when lines of people began to form, saying, "We need bread." We could not say, "Go, be thou filled." If there were six small loaves and a few fishes, we had to divide them. There was always bread.
> We were just sitting there talking and people moved in on us.

Let those who can take it, take it. Some moved out and that made room for more. And somehow the walls expanded.

We were just sitting there talking and someone said, "Let's go live on a farm."

It was as casual as all that, I often think. It just came about. It just happened.

I found myself, a barren woman, the joyful mother of children. It is not easy always to be joyful, to keep in mind the duty of delight.

The most significant thing about *The Catholic Worker* is poverty, some say.

The most significant thing is community, others say. We are not alone anymore.

But the final word is love. At times it has been, in the words of Father Zossima, a harsh and dreadful thing, and our very faith in love has been tried by fire.

We cannot love God unless we love each other, and to love we must know each other. We know Him in the breaking of bread, and we are not alone anymore. Heaven is a banquet and life is a banquet, too, even with a crust, where there is companionship.

We have all known the loneliness and we have learned that the only solution is love and that love comes with community.

It all happened while we sat there talking, and it is still going on.

The long pilgrimage of Dorothy Day still testifies to the same simple things with which she began: to refuse to kill, to serve the poor, to give one's life to compassion and love. She had been a loving adversary of every political regime under which she had lived. Hers was a radical position. It is such a position which ultimately has the greatest historic significance. Other responses—more moderate, more reasonable, more responsive to political reality—are always more tied to the culture, and will therefore die with it.

The influence of people like Dorothy Day always trickles in from outside the cultural mainstream. Yet it seems that lives like hers are the ones which affect the culture most, certainly more than those lives comfortably bordered by the values and structures of their society. She remained convinced that the way to build a new society is to build it in your own life, in the situation in which you find yourself. Her vision was a new society growing up within the shell of the old.

Dorothy Day died on Saturday night, November 29, 1980. She was eighty-three. Dorothy died in her room at Maryhouse, a place of hospitality she founded for homeless women on New York's Lower East Side.

I always thought I would go to her funeral. I met her only twice, but no one affected me like she did. I was on the road when I heard, and it was too late to get to the service.

The feeling of grief was overwhelming. She embodied everything I believe in. She, more than any other, made my faith seem real and possible to live. She took my most cherished visions and made them into realities. Now she was gone. It was like the end of an era.

Slowly, the grief gave way to gratitude. We were richly blessed to have had her among us, if only for a while. She was an ordinary woman whose faith caused her to do extraordinary things. The gospel caught fire in this woman and caused an explosion of love. We will miss her like a part of ourselves.

The doctors said that she died of heart failure. But Dorothy's heart never failed us.

. . . .

I suppose my knowledge of St. Francis was like most people's. If someone had asked me, an evangelical kid from Detroit, "Who was the most famous saint?" I would have puzzled for a moment and probaly ended up by saying, "Oh, yes, St. Francis." If that person had then asked me what I know about the famous saint, I would certainly have been stumped and, at best, come up with something about him loving birds and nature. St. Francis of the birdbath endures as one of the worst caricatures of history.

Years of university and seminary education did little to correct my shallow impression of the little poor man of Assisi.

(Protestant seminaries generally don't do very well with the lives of saints.) It wasn't until a few years ago, when I had the rare commodity of a free evening, that I had my first real exposure to Francis. *Brother Sun, Sister Moon,* the movie produced by Franco Zeffirelli, was playing for a dollar at our local cheap movie theater on a double bill with *Romeo and Juliet.* I had seen the teen-age romance before, but had heard that the other was good.

I was completely unprepared for my first meeting with the saint. It was the beginning of an intense and often painful friendship, one that has affected me profoundly.

Now, after studying the life of Francis, the movie seems quite inadequate, with an unnecessarily romantic and ethereal quality. The real Francis, I think, was much more human and powerful than Zeffirelli's fragile and otherworldly character. But despite the film's limitations, this introduction to Francis left me overwhelmed with emotion.

I left the theater stunned and speechless. On the way home in the dark car, I quietly began to weep. Never before had I encountered a life so consumed with the gospel, a man so on fire with the love of God, a disciple so single-mindedly focused on following after Jesus, a spirit so joyful in abandoning everything to serve his Lord. The evangelical poverty of Francis had evangelized me to the depths of my soul.

I immediately began to question everything about my life. His utter obedience to Christ was radiant in exposing the places where my commitment was still compromised. His intimacy with God created in me what the monks call "a holy jealousy." His wholehearted love for Jesus Christ made me love our Master more than I ever had before. Francis was converting me again to Jesus. I cried that night because my faith seemed so small and weak when compared to his. I wondered what my life was counting for.

It's so easy to be a "radical Christian" in America. Here the church is so affluent, so comfortable, so lukewarm, that the most basic kind of discipleship or the simplest acts of justice, mercy, and peace seem extraordinary by comparison. Living what should be just an ordinary Christian life is enough to be designated radical by a spiritually impoverished church.

It is a constant temptation to accept the designation and, worse yet, to allow the American church to become the standard by which we measure ourselves. For Francis, the standard was always Christ and Christ alone, not the thirteenth-century church, nor even the movement of renewal that he founded.

G. K. Chesterton wrote of him: "So soon as he certainly has followers, he does not compare himself with his followers, towards whom he might appear as a master; he compares himself more and more with his Master, towards whom he appears only as a servant."

That simple insight articulated by Chesterton struck deep within me that night. What is the measure of my life? How have I let the standard of others make me complacent to the standard of Christ? I felt a hunger in me for what I saw in this little man from Assisi.

What I saw was Christ vividly incarnate in the life of Francis. It was like meeting Jesus afresh.

My struggle with the testimony of Francis has grown. On a retreat, I read several of his biographies. Again I felt drawn closer to Jesus than at any time since my conversion and the founding of Sojourners. I came home with a deepening love for the humble saint and a growing desire for a closer walk with Christ.

Since then, Francis has been the subject of more reading, a cause of much reflection, a catalyst for prayer, a push for deeper self-examination.

Francis did not merely accept poverty, he pursued it. Some want to be poor for reasons of philosophy, ideology, or asceticism. Francis wanted to be poor because Jesus was poor and because his beloved Master so loved the poor. In other words, Francis stressed poverty so strongly, not for its own sake, but in order to become closer to God and nearer to the forgotten and the suffering ones of the earth.

"Love for the poor was born in him," wrote St. Bonaventure. He virtually reveled in poverty and took the greatest joy in destitution. The great love affair between Francis and his "Lady Poverty" rivals all the most famous romances of history.

For Francis, poverty without humiliation was no gain. "What is the use of renouncing the riches of the earth, if you intend to keep those of self-love?" he used to say to his friars.

One day one of the brothers asked Francis why everyone seemed to be running after him. "Why after you?" he asked several times, pointing out that Francis was neither handsome, noble, or wise. Francis answered:

> I have this from the all-holy eyes of God that see the good and the evil everywhere. For those blessed and all-holy eyes have not seen among sinners anyone more vile or insufficient than I am. And so in order to do that wonderful work which he intends to do, he did not find on earth a more ordinary creature, and therefore he chose me. For God has chosen the foolish things of this world to put to shame the wise, and God has chosen the base things of this world and the despised, to bring to naught the noble, the great, and the strong (*The Little Flowers of St. Francis*, Raphael Brown).

He called his brothers Friars Minor, which means the little, unimportant ones. But for Francis humility was not a virtue to be sought after; rather, it was the natural result of a heart overflowing with the worship of God and the most profound respect and affection for every creature God had made.

Never has God been so freely praised nor ordinary men and women so highly regarded as in the life of Francis. His was a spiritual populism rooted in the love of God.

Chesterton reflects on this point:

> What gave him his extraordinary personal power was this: that from the Pope to the beggar, from the sultan of Syria in his pavilion to the ragged robbers crawling out of the wood, there was never a man who looked into those brown burning eyes without being certain that Francis Bernardone was really interested in *him*; in his own inner individual life from the

cradle to the grave; that he himself was being valued and taken seriously, and not merely added to the spoils of some social policy or the names in some clerical document. . . . We may say if we like that St. Francis, in the bare and barren simplicity of his life, had clung to one rag of luxury: the manners of a court. But whereas in a court there is one king and a hundred courtiers, in this story there was one courtier, moving among a hundred kings. For he treated the whole mob of men as a mob of kings (*St. Francis of Assisi*, Chesterton).

Francis received his vocation before the wooden crucifix of the abandoned church of San Damiano: "Francis, go repair my house, which is falling into ruins." To see the church restored to Christ was his driving passion and the heart of his calling. Like every authentic renewal movement in the history of the church, the Franciscan revolution was simply a return to the gospel, and Francis of Assisi returned to the gospel with such force that it shook the entire world.

Even Vladimir Lenin bowed in respect to the faith, thought, and life of Francis:

> I made a mistake. Without doubt, an oppressed multitude had to be liberated. But our method only provoked further oppression and atrocious massacres. My living nightmare is to find myself lost in an ocean of red with the blood of innumerable victims. It is too late now to alter the past, but what was needed to save Russia were ten Francis of Assisi's (*Letters on Modern Atheism*, Vladimir Ilyich Lenin).

The church always wanted Francis to write a rule for his order, as the leaders of all the other orders had done. But he always felt the gospel was enough.

One day Francis and some of the brothers set out at dawn for the Church of San Nicolo to hear Mass. They opened the gospel three times at random. The first time, their eyes fell on these words: "If you will be perfect, go, sell what you have, and give to the poor." The second time, they read: "Take nothing for your journey"; and the third time: "If anyone wishes to come after Me, let him deny himself, and take up the cross, and follow Me."

"Here," said Francis, "is what we are going to do, and all those who shall afterwards join us" (*St. Francis of Assisi*, Englebert).

Those simple gospel imperatives became the basis for the Franciscan way of life and the foundation of the first Rule of 1209. Francis' rules were simply the repetition of gospel texts with some commentary and guidelines for regulating the life of the friars. The Sermon on the Mount would have sufficed as Francis' rule, if he had had his way.

The desire of Francis and his brothers to live without property and security was always resisted by the church. The story of their first trip to Rome to gain acceptance of their order raised the central problem:

> Thus all were of the opinion that so literal an interpretation of the Gospel went beyond human strength, and the Pope himself declared, "Although your zeal, my dear sons, reassures us, we must nevertheless think of your successors, who may find the path you wish to follow too austere."
>
> But the Cardinal of St. Paul replied, "If we reject this poor man's request on such a pretext, would not this be to declare that the Gospel cannot be practiced, and so to blaspheme Christ, its Author?" (Englebert).

At the heart of Christian faith is the incarnation. Abstract talk about God has always left me empty and longing for more. I need God made flesh, human like us, walking our streets, even in our shoes, teaching us the way to live. I also need people who teach me again the reality of the incarnation in their own lives and history.

Francis is perhaps our greatest teacher. He has been called both "the first Christian" and "the last Christian." My struggle is just that; his life presents the gospel in such stark contrast to the world, to the church, and to my life. Sometimes his example convinces me that it is indeed possible, with God's abundant grace, to live the gospel life. Other times his star shines so bright that it only exposes my own darkness. Francis converts me over and over to Jesus, but he also makes me sometimes wonder if I really am or want to be a Christian. He both points to the great possibility and shows me how much further I have to go to see what he saw.

To follow after him as he dances through the world will certainly turn one's life upside down. To walk with Francis, even a little way, is a great adventure, but also a painful one. It is a journey that I still find myself very much in the middle of.

I don't know where the journey will end. But I do know that once you have looked into the eyes of Francis, you will never see the same again.

10
Revival

In the fifteenth year of the reign of Tiberius Caesar, Pontius Pilate being governor of Judea, and Herod being tetrarch of Galilee, and his brother Philip tetrarch of the region of Ituraea and Trachonitis, and Lysanias tetrarch of Abilene, in the high-priesthood of Annas and Caiaphas, the word of God came to John the son of Zechariah in the wilderness. (Luke 3:1-2)

This passage is one of my favorites among the ironic gems that fill the Bible. It is about the location of the Word of God. Following the list of powerful, important people of the day, both political and religious, we are told that the Word of God came to John in the wilderness.

The Word of God is located outside the centers of power, and one must leave them to hear it. Jesus was baptized and tempted in the desert. And after his time of testing he returned with a mission to preach the kingdom of God. The message was the same as that of John and the Old Testament prophets before him. The message was, in a word, repent.

Our great cultural joke is the bearded religious fanatic in weird dress carrying a sign with the words, "Repent, the end is near." Perhaps we laugh at that man because we are afraid of his message. Salvation in America will mean to repent of America.

Today, American Christians have fled the wilderness. They seek the Word of God in the centers of power, at prayer breakfasts with political rulers. They seek salvation and legitimation without repentance.

I come from the evangelical tradition. Evangelicals are becoming more and more at ease in the land; born-again religion is everywhere. All of the attention can give the impression that there is a revival at hand. But the biblical authenticity of such a "revival" must be probed.

Evangelicals are welcoming society's recognition with an embrace of their own. The new evangelical embrace of America includes a sense that success, acceptance, and respect in this society should come naturally to Christians, and that conversion ought to produce these fruits.

Conversion has become a highly personal matter which helps one get along better in America, and the spread of personal piety has become the standard by which to judge the nation's morality. The characteristics of the gospel that are least marketable—self-sacrifice, servanthood, the way of the cross, identification with the poor, a prophetic witness to the state, a life of simplicity and sharing, justice and peace—are the gospel values that don't get communicated to the society when the media explains what being born again is all about.

The use of evangelical Christians, evangelical churches, and evangelical religion by American political leaders for their own purposes is a practice that is as politically common as it is spiritually despicable. All too often, evangelicals have been happy to be used. In return for uncritical support and religious affirmation of American economic and political goals, evangelicals have received cultural acceptance, economic prosperity, and access to political power. It is an old historical pattern for leading American evangelists to be bankrolled by leading American businessmen and courted by leading American politicians, producing a gospel that is palatable to the rich and powerful.

I was recently invited to a meeting on what the churches could do to help the poor in their current crisis. The meeting was held on the day of the National Prayer Breakfast (an occasion which I have religiously avoided). Against my better judgment, but out of a favor to a friend, I decided to go. On hand were assorted Christian leaders who that morning had attended the breakfast, which has become a time to honor the president and give him a chance to justify in religious terms what he is doing. I feel that when the president mets with Christian leaders it ought to be a time for biblical accountablity and prophetic witness, not mutual affirmation.

The meeting to talk about the poor was held where the prayer breakfast had been, at the Sheraton Washington Hotel (a familiar place for me by now) in a chandeliered, carpeted ballroom. No poor people were there.

Two members of the White House staff showed up for the meeting. They were, of course, born-again Christians like all the rest of us and were simply there as "brothers." It was pretty clear to me that someone had a plan, and that we were all about to be invited to become part of it. The dialogue, or rather monologue, from the Reagan administration evangelicals which followed was extraordinary and bears a public retelling. To the best of my recollection, here is how it went.

One of the two began:

> Now that the government is getting out of providing welfare for the poor, which it never should have done anyway, the churches can get involved, which they should have been doing all along. We have a tremendous opportunity here. Ronald Reagan has cleared the way for the church to take up the challenge.
>
> You remember the biblical pattern of the prophet speaking to the king. Well, now the king has a word for the prophets. If we could just unite the efforts of the churches with those of our major corporations, it could be the greatest example of voluntarism we've ever seen. [I knew someone would use that word.]

More followed:

> We need a spiritual revival in this country. If that revival happens, we are prepared to coordinate things through the White House Task Force on Private Initiative. The president is prepared to put the moral authority of the presidency behind this effort.

And:

> I want you to know the president really cares about poor people. He actually can't sleep at night for fear that some people might fall through the safety net. This president cares. Now, the poor don't realize that he cares. That's why it's our job to convince them that he really does care. If people would just not be so critical of the president and what he is trying to do, if people would just give him some praise for his efforts, it would make a lot of difference. For example, if *Sojourners* would just not be so negative about our policies and offer some real support. . . .

The White House representative finished talking and said he was sorry to leave so quickly but he had another appointment.

Had this conversation taken place on 14th Street, it would have been a bad joke. Meetings like this can only happen in nice hotels far removed from the people who are the subject of the conversation. With very high-sounding words, the poor were patronized, the government let off the hook, and the rich and powerful upheld as the saviors of the unfortunate. The churches were being invited to join with the nation's business leaders to solve "the problem of the poor." The meeting itself was a classic example of why the poor have problems.

I was almost overwhelmed with anger, though I felt more like crying than cursing. All I could do was repeat the words of Mary's "Magnificat" from Luke 1 to remind the other representative from the Reagan administration that if a revival does happen in this country the people now in control will be put out of power, the lowly will be lifted up, the hungry filled with good things, and the rich sent empty away.

The meeting ended in disarray. I don't know if there have been any more meetings. I haven't been invited.

Some evangelical preachers and strategists claim credit for the victory of Ronald Reagan. Whether or not their influence was decisive is less important than is their public identification with that new regime and its nationalistic vision for America's future. Their enormous support and energy expended on behalf of the political Right has now saddled them with responsibility for the results of the 1980 elections.

As an evangelical, I am deeply grieved by the image presented to the public by the television preachers and their New Right allies. The superpatriotism of their movement flies in the face of the biblical vision of the people of God who know no national boundaries but live among the nations as ministers of reconciliation. They are joining and perpetuating the national frenzy of fear and hostility toward our adversaries and calling for an increasing military buildup in a world already on the brink of total destruction.

While many evangelicals may not be comfortable with the right-wing extremism of some of evangelicalism's more public and vocal figures, most are still at home somewhere in the middle of the road, though toward the slow, right lane of it. They choose the same style of life as most of their neighbors and earn respect as solid citizens, shedding themselves of the minority status their ancestors knew.

The American church is in danger of losing any sense of its true identity. The New Testament vision of the kingdom of God has been easily replaced by an American civil religion in which the church's life has become so wedded to the realities of the present American order that the sense of preserving the holy, of bearing witness to the evangel, of living under the Word of God, is lost.

Contrary to the record of the early church, the American church suffers not from persecution, but from seduction, both by the culture and the state. The vision of a "Christian America" held by a growing number in the United States means the sacrifice of the radical demands of the gospel.

The notion so popular after World War II of God's purposes and America's destiny being one and the same has reemerged with new vigor in the proclamations of the television preachers and their political allies of the New Right. A few months ago, I was in a dialogue at a conference of the National Association of Evangelicals on the question of nuclear war. My dialogue partner was a brigadier general who was also an Episcopal priest. He proudly proclaimed to a room full of evangelical Christians that America has a crucial role in the fulfillment of the Great Commission. He unashamedly tied the destiny of the American nation with the purposes of God in history.

However, Pax Americana is over. Our defeat in Vietnam showed that events are no longer in our control. Revolutionary forces are at work in the world among the masses of the poor and the oppressed, and America increasingly shows itself to be on the wrong side of their struggle. While superior fire power continues to be on our side, justice is clearly on the side of those who are struggling for the most rudimentary elements of human freedom and dignity.

The church must recover the message of Matthew 25: the place of Jesus is with the poor and marginal people, living on the edge, in economic insecurity. This is the desert today.

No image is less attractive to most of us than that of the desert: barren, stark, without comforts or security. Men and women once went to the wilderness to seek God. In the desert, God's love and grace must be sufficient. Now we have abandoned the search for God, and the wilderness is in us.

Even many who have shown their opposition to the system, slowly, over time, make small compromises with it and make their peace with the established order. So deep is our need for comfort and security that when our souls are not filled with the relentless pursuit of God, that need will always fill the empty spaces.

The prophetic tradition suggests that things look clearer from the margins. The biblical insight is usually an outsider's insight. The church is meant to be a marginal community in whatever circumstance it finds itself—marginal because of its loyalty to Jesus Christ.

To be marginal in one's society is not, emphatically not, to withdraw, as some would charge. It is to be motivated and led by values and commitments different from and often contrary to the mainstream. It is to have the capacity of bringing something new and fresh to the public arena.

New vision is always what any society most needs, and the edges of society have always been the most likely place for it to emerge. To generate something new, one must be listening to voices other than the loud voices of a mass society.

To be on the margins, therefore, is to put ourselves in a position to watch, to listen, and to become engaged in a new way. To look from the margins usually enables us to see better what is to be done and perhaps to know better how to go about it. In other words, being closer to the edges than the mainstream yields perspective.

Part of being on the margins is new association with the people who have been made marginal. The gospel tells us that it is among "the least of these" where we find Jesus.

I remember a midweek community worship during Advent in which association with the marginal became the theme of our sharing. Dan Goering began by saying, "This week I've met Jesus fifty times." He spoke out of his work with Salvadoran refugees, trying to get them settled in Washington with housing and enough work to survive. He had heard countless stories of children, parents, husbands, and wives murdered by the military security forces in El Salvador, of separated families, of fear for loved ones left behind. Said Dan, "I can scarcely believe their composure, their faith, their hopeful spirit. When I told one woman that there was simply no work to be found, she thanked me, smiled, reached in her pocket and handed me a dollar for our work." I bowed my head and pondered how much the poor can teach the rich about generosity.

Judi Floyd, a nurse at a neighborhood medical clinic, sadly reported that an old street man who had come regularly to the clinic froze to death the night before in an abandoned garage. The hurt and pain she felt at losing a friend in such a brutal way quickly went around the room. "People have a right not to freeze to death," someone cried. But another old street gentleman had come back to the clinic today, she reported. For the first time, he had allowed Judi to unwrap his layers of clothing—three coats, six shirts, and several ties—to rub medicine on his raw back. "Never has rubbing anyone's back meant so much to me. It was, for me, like anointing Jesus."

As we gathered around the Eucharist, the tears of the community were released for the people of Poland. It had been a rough week, a time of listening and waiting for reports about what was occurring. I realized how much hope I had invested in the birth and growth of Solidarity. The reports of Lech Walesa "broken and weeping" were more than I could take.

Oh, how fragile are our hopes for justice, for peace, for life. Dashed hopes, outlawed unions, martial law in Warsaw and San Salvador, murdered loved ones and families made refugees, frozen street people—these were the hard facts of our Advent. And so we waited, Advent style. How long, O Lord? Must our waiting slip into despair?

We celebrated the Eucharist that night, and we saw the fragility of God in Jesus Christ, broken bread, poured-out wine. But here was the key, the hope of the world. There is nothing to do but unite our fragile lives with his and know that through him the world will be saved.

What else can we do in the face of so many made marginal? Shall we give up, give in, pull back? What do they need? Not for us to shrink from their pain and withdraw to despair because of their suffering. But rather to see, because of how great their suffering, how much more we need to love.

Perhaps the only difference between hope and despair is going on. Werner Koch, a pastor of the Confessing Church in Germany during Hitler's regime who spent two years in a Nazi concentration camp, told this story to me while visiting our community:

> In the concentration camps we found every morning five, six, seven, eight comrades hanging on the electrical barbed wire, because during the night they came out of the barracks full of despair and put an end to their lives. I confess that I also had many moments of despair, because every morning when you woke up you couldn't know if you would be alive in the evening. We had to bear witness to so many cruelties and assassinations during the day. We were physically so strained and helpless that danger of resignation was very close at times.

But there was a voice we couldn't forget. The voice said, "Don't be anxious; I have overcome the world. I am the resurrection and the life." And so we said to each other that we are on the side of victory. It is not the wicked, not the evil, who have the last word. So we received from day to day the courage to go on.

When overwhelmed with the reality of suffering, we can decide either not to feel it or let ourselves take it in. If we take it in, we will either succumb to despair or be moved to a greater depth of love, which is to come closer to God. There are no other choices. We will either curse the darkness, or we will say, "Come, Lord Jesus, we need you now more than ever."

As Christians become identified with the marginal people, we too will become marginalized, pushed to the edges of society. We too will inhabit the desert, in opposition to things as they are, in solidarity with the poor, in solitude and prayer, in community, in prison, in risk-taking and sacrifice. Key to the church's recovery of its identity is its relinquishment of privilege and control—being willing to risk its position and even social legitimacy for the sake of the gospel.

The vital relationships between sacrifice and change, suffering and liberation, crucifixion and resurrection become evident to a church that decides to live out a theology that is truly incarnational. Jesus offered to the Father a loving prayer for his disciples, spoken shortly before his death:

> 'And now I am coming to thee; but while I am still in the world I speak these words, so that they may have my joy within them in full measure. I have delivered thy word to them, and the world hates them because they are strangers in the world, as I am. I pray thee, not to take them out of the world, but to keep them from the evil one. They are strangers in the world, as I am. Consecrate them by the truth; thy word is truth. As thou hast sent me into the world, I have sent them into the world, and for their sake I now consecrate myself, that they too may be consecrated by the truth.
>
> 'But it is not for these alone that I pray, but for those also who through their words put their faith in me' (John 17:13-20 NEB).

Jesus here prays for his disciples and for all those who come after them. He knows that they will be in conflict with the world. He knows this because his own life, his words, his kingdom were in such conflict, and now his life is in them, his words have been received by them, and the message of his kingdom has been entrusted to them. The world will treat them as they treated him.

I was once speaking at a Christian college, where in the course of my talk I asked, "Why was Jesus killed?" A long pause followed, indicating that the question was one that had not been thought about much before. Finally, an answer came, "To save us from our sins."

True enough as to the result of Jesus' death, but I was asking about the cause. Why was Jesus killed?

It is quite doubtful that the chief priests who collaborated with Pontius Pilate to accomplish the execution were conscious of their part in salvation history. What they were conscious of was that Jesus was a threat to their power and authority.

Jesus frequently had confrontations with these rulers of the people, treating them with disdain and scorn, on one occasion calling Herod a "fox." He spared no words in his criticism of the rich and powerful and on one occasion he specifically condemned the kings of the Gentiles, who sought power and dominated their subjects while calling themselves "benefactors."

He contrasted his own approach to power with that of the secular rulers and called upon his disciples to imitate, not them, but his own servant style of leadership. Jesus, in fact, told his disciples to expect persecution from political authorities on his account, and he instructed them in how to bear witness when they are "brought before kings and governors for my name's sake."

Jesus' cleansing of the temple was a flagrant act of civil disobedience aimed at the religious, economic, and political power center of the established order. The temple symbolized the power of the ruling authorities. Jesus acted directly against their authority by accusing them of corrupting the worship of the temple and by challenging their economic base: "My house shall be a house of prayer. . . . But you have made it a den of robbers" (Mark 11:17).

Jesus' anger is clear in the scene's description. He took direct public action, and his behavior was bold and startling to all those around. Jesus' action was deeply political and a fundamental challenge to the economy of the temple. The temple authorities recognized a frontal assault on the religious and political establishment and demanded that Jesus explain what his authority was for doing such a thing. Jesus, using the image of the temple itself, pointed to his own resurrection as his authority. That temple action sparked a chain of events which led to his crucifixion.

But Jesus not only confronted the reigning authorities directly. His new order undermined the entire system upon which their rule was based. This new order, which relied on the power of suffering and servanthood rather than violence and domination, represented a profound threat to the leaders of the establishment. It was such a threat, in fact, that they killed him.

Jesus' clash with the ruling religious and political authorities of his day surely has a message for us. Yet the idea that the gospel lives in conflict with the ruling axioms and authorities of the American nation still sends tremors through a church that has fought so hard to achieve majority status. We still want to make the gospel compatible with our cultural desires and loyalties. But we can't.

Most of us have yet to fully realize the enormous distance between the culture to which we are so tied and the gospel we espouse. We have greatly underestimated the disruption and struggle that genuine conversion will occasion in our lives.

A gathering last year of sixty people from Christian communities across the country graphically illustrated the point. Over the past five years a close relationship between a broadly ecumenical circle of communities has developed; this was our winter meeting.

Here were people who were more than "just interested" in

the gospel. Those assembled had already made some serious choices. They had already given up lucrative jobs and promising careers, relinquished rights to houses and property, and were living on the edge of economy insecurity. They had moved in to share life closely with other people, opened their families to the needs of others, relocated to live among the poor, become involved in the struggles of those around them, and begun a labor for justice and peace which was leading to inevitable confrontation with political authorities.

They had set their feet on a new path, and it was costing them a lot. Many changes had taken place in their lives. All those present had begun to establish new patterns of living in their personal, family, economic, vocational, and political lives. For most of the eleven communities represented, it had been a year of struggle and pain.

They had seriously set about to live the gospel and had run into a common experience—the taste of suffering. And they knew it had just begun. These community leaders had radically altered the more normal course their lives might otherwise have taken. The result was often insecurity and loneliness.

From the first day of the meeting, the sharing of suffering and pain became the common and unifying experience. The choices we had made caused us all to feel vulnerable and exposed—to our weakness and sin, to one another, and to the hostility of a culture completely set against the course of life we have chosen in the gospel.

During the days together, we were given the grace to share our broken places with one another. Never have I experienced a clearer demonstration of strength coming out of weakness, faith coming out of struggle, joy coming out of suffering. There was little need for long explanations of why things had been so hard. Everyone knew.

We were hungry for teaching, for fellowship, and especially for worship. We held a service of intercession for one another one evening that lasted long into the night. We wanted to be together; we needed to be together.

Out of that time came a deep renewal of faith. Our prayers

erupted into joyous dancing and singing at one-thirty in the morning. The taste of suffering had made us hungry, and we were deeply fed. The clear word that came during the last Eucharist was "stay hungry."

The experience brought to mind both the history of the early Christians, who spent may hours together in prayer and intimate worship, and the stories of Third-World Christians today who gather all night in their churches and homes when crisis is threatening.

The message was that suffering is the natural consequence of living the gospel; joy and strength are the fruits of suffering for the sake of Christ. Perhaps the most grievous thing about the American churches today is the absence of suffering and struggle. It is in fact our fear of suffering that has extinguished the possibility of real joy.

It is a great mystery, this relationship between suffering and joy, weakness and strength. But to those who have known it, it has been the deepest of all human experiences.

We are invited to follow after Jesus as he heads toward Jerusalem, to enter into his sufferings and to feel the power of his resurrection. It has never made sense. But the truth of it has been confirmed in the experience of Christians since the beginning who have been willing to take the risk. A faith refined by fire is the testimony of all Christians who now suffer for the sake of the gospel.

Our security has taken away our appetite for the gospel. Entering the sufferings of Christ in our own situation offers the American church its only real future. The time is rapidly approaching when we will no longer be able to avoid this reality. To avoid the path of suffering is to remain ignorant of Jesus; to embrace it is to learn intimacy with Christ.

Central to middle-class existence in America is the avoidance of pain, hardship, and suffering. The sacrifice that has been a way of life for older generations and for much of the world's population today is to most of us alien and fearful. We assume that we have a right to be protected from it.

But Peter says to us,

Beloved, do not be surprised at the fiery ordeal which comes upon you to prove you, as though something strange were happening to you. But rejoice in so far as you share Christ's sufferings, that you may also rejoice and be glad when his glory is revealed. If you are reproached for the name of Christ, you are blessed, because the spirit of glory and of God rests upon you (I Pet. 4:12-14).

The relationship between our identity with Christ's suffering and participation in his glory is crucial. The New Testament assumption is that to follow Christ in the world will bring suffering. Certainly the early church knew this to be true. But persecution did not weaken its faith, as the authorities had hoped. It had quite the opposite effect, as we have seen again and again in the world's most persecuted places, where faith flourishes. Paul reflects in his letter to the Romans on the situation of the early believers:

Who shall separate us from the love of Christ? Shall tribulation, or distress, or persecution, or famine, or nakedness, or peril, or sword? As it is written,

"For thy sake we are being killed all the day long; we are regarded as sheep to be slaughtered."

No, in all these things we are more than conquerors through him who loved us. For I am sure that neither death, nor life, nor angels, nor principalities, nor things present, nor things to come, nor powers, nor height, nor depth, nor anything else in all creation, will be able to separate us from the love of God in Christ Jesus our Lord (Rom. 8:35-39).

This remarkable and uplifting passage describes the unshakable promise of God. The context of these verses is important. Paul assumes that weakness, conflict, and hardship are normal for the Christian life and, for that matter, human life.

The goal of American Christianity is to get out of adversity and into security. We believe in the God of the quick fix who will make us happy, prosperous, and protected. This is a false gospel.

For Paul adversity is part of life, and especially part of the

Christian life lived in conflict with the world. Success, according to this passage, is not the avoidance of adversity but knowing the love of God in adversity. The promise made by the passage is not that God will remove the difficulties of life, but that God will continue to love us through them.

Those who accept the adversities of life and find God's love in the midst of them are those who become the wise, healed, whole, and joyful people. Often Christians whose faith has been purified through suffering are the most joyful of all. On the other hand, those who spend their lives in the desperate attempt to avoid hardship and pain often end up most miserable and filled with anxiety.

Our comfortable Christian lives in the United States, which are seldom in conflict with the world, make it difficult for us to understand this passage. But it is beginning to make sense to those Christians who are making their way into community, into relationships with the poor, into economic insecurity, into peacemaking. We have begun to experience some of what Paul is talking about; to know our own and others' weakness, fear, pain, conflict, struggle, and persecution by the authorities. This is a passage for our future.

It speaks now to circumstances of the church in Central America, Poland, and elsewhere, but it is for our future as we respond more faithfully to the gospel and join in active fellowship with the suffering church in other parts of the world. That is the key to our future.

Suffering does not necessarily lead to spiritual maturity. It can lead to bitterness, frustration, anger, and violence. We all know people who have allowed their suffering to embitter them and destroy their lives. Even social movements in response to injustice and suffering can become violent forces of revenge and hatred.

But oppression and suffering can also lead to trust in the love of God. Suffering can help us let go of everything and realize that there is no alternative but to depend on God. Abandoning ourselves to the love of God leads to spiritual maturity and wisdom.

We see both responses in ourselves, others, and in places of great oppression that have become revolutionary situations. The first response will always destroy, the second one will heal.

The passage is simply the promise of God, whether we feel it or not. Whether we accept it or not it is our choice.

I am convinced, says Paul, that nothing can separate us from the love of God in Christ Jesus. We, too, must become convinced of that. It is, in the end, the one thing we can hang onto in a world that is in deep crisis.

The nation moves from one crisis to another so fast that the word has become a description of our whole way of life. The economy is rapidly being destroyed by the twin devils of unemployment and inflation. Our water becomes dirtier, our air harder to breathe, and our land poisoned—all from the massive wastes of a consumer society. Even our bodies show the consequences of a polluted environment, as one out of every four of us is afflicted with cancer, the plague of a technological age. The resources of our finite world are reaching their limits as we who were charged to be stewards have instead been exploiters, creating whole populations doomed to poverty.

It is a period of political withdrawal and instability. Politicians are suspect. Only half of those people eligible in the last presidential election even bothered to vote. The standard reason: "It doesn't make any difference." The major institutions of government, business, and labor generate no confidence. Corruption is assumed on every level by a cynical public. Self-interest and apathy are the two poles of public life.

It is a time of insecurity and spiritual decay. Our low value for human life is evident both in escalating military expenditures and rising abortion rates. Crime runs out of control in the streets and in corporate boardrooms and corridors of power. Sexual values reflect the selfishness of a consumer society whose watchwords are always "more" and "better." Personal gratification replaces commitment and undermines the integrity of marriage, family, and the whole notion of relationships based on covenants.

It is a time of transition. And in such an era, many solutions will be offered. Some people will seek desperately to hang on to the status quo. Those who profit most from the existing order will fight with all their might against any change that would deprive them of their wealth and power.

But for those of us who follow a Lord who showed us the way of the cross, who know that even times of greatest crisis cannot separate us from our God, there is another option.

I have been told that the Chinese symbol for crisis combines the two symbols for danger and opportunity. For some of us who see the danger of these times, there is also vision to see the opportunity for a true spiritual revival. Because the present crisis has so much to do with our basic spiritual values, the possibility of revival is great.

At similar times of crisis, when social problems defined themselves as overriding moral issues, evangelical Christians have responded, and in many cases led movements for change. The slavery question was such an issue in the nineteenth century. The abolitionist movement had its roots deep in revivalist soil. People like Charles Finney, Theodore Weld, Jonathan Blanchard, A. J. Gordon, the Grimké sisters, and the Tappan brothers are known not only as abolitionist leaders, but also as outstanding revivalist leaders. Their fervent preaching and social agitation are the background of today's evangelical movement, though one would never know it by observing the current state of the evangelical world. The biblical demands for justice and righteousness so close to the hearts of the nineteenth-century evangelicals have been all but forgotten by their twentieth-century descendants.

The evangelical tradition, contrary to our experience of its cultural captivity, has the capacity to fundamentally challenge the American status quo and offer a desperately needed vision of justice and peace firmly rooted in the Bible. While the state will continue to try to keep evangelical faith a civil religion, a growing number of us find that our biblical faith makes us increasingly uncivil in regard to the present political and economic order.

There has always been a very basic contradiction at the heart of America's use and abuse of biblical Christian faith to serve its national purposes. I believe the day is upon us in which that contradiction is being exposed. Indeed, a revival of genuine biblical faith in this country might in fact be the one thing that could most undermine the injustice and violence that have become endemic to the American system.

Historically, revival has been directed to the need for basic change in our lives and our society. The connection between conversion and participation in God's historical purposes is the key to genuine revival. A new American revival could be the very thing leading to the transformation of spiritual values that so many have now suggested we desperately need if we are to survive our present crisis and go on to better possibilities.

America has long sought to justify itself in Christian terms. That practice may come back to haunt the leaders of church and state as we witness Christians whose opposition to illegitimate power is based on their relationship to Jesus Christ and whose protest is cast in specifically biblical terms. A whole new generation of Christians may turn American's affirmation of the biblical heritage on its head.

It is the biblical seeds of protest, political resistance, and alternative vision that could most threaten the present American status quo. A radical revivalism that is biblically based and sprung from the churches could be a far more serious threat to the established order in America than mere political responses rooted in secular ideologies.

In Ephesians, Paul tells us that our fight with the principalities and powers and with spiritual wickedness in high places is a spiritual warfare. That means we need to experience even more deeply the power of the Spirit in active combat with the powers that be. There is no telling how much tremendous new energy and power would be released by a prayerful movement of Christians who felt themselves to be totally dependent on the power and the presence of the Holy Spirit. We need to pray for it, watch for it, listen for it, prepare for it, and be open to it when it comes.

The creation of truly confessing communities is crucial to

the recovery of the church's lost identity. Confessing Christ in ways that are authentic and biblically faithful will emerge as the daily existence of the Christian community becomes a countersign to American wealth and power.

A new spirit is blowing in the churches. The resurgence of a confessing community in the United States has already begun. The key to it is the integration of spiritual and social renewal. This radical renewal which is now ocurring in the American churches is based on Bible study, worship, prayer, recovery of pastoral life, and a renewal of the Holy Spirit from which is flowing a new sense of social mission and political resistance.

Here, there, and everywhere, communities are rising up like leaven with a message that offers genuine hope for our times. New relationships and alignments in the churches centering on a radical response to Christ and the call to community are coming together. A new and very ecumenical movement is emerging from diverse traditions and streams.

How far the present awakening might spread, how deep it will go into the church's life, what enduring changes will come about, and how it might affect the future are questions that are as yet unanswered. But the new stirring among Christians is undeniable.

As I reflect on my own life in the midst of this exciting awakening, I realize that I have come full circle. I have begun to understand the separation and alienation of my younger years, and I feel myself wanting to return to the roots of my own tradition.

My love for the church has grown. My anger at the control of the system over the church has deepened, but my desire now is less to condemn the church for its conformity and more to see a captive church set free.

My vocation has grown more clear over the years as well. I enjoy being an editor, but have never really felt like a journalist. I realize that, more than anything else, I am a preacher and a pastor at heart. I wear many other hats—theologian, author, activist, organizer. They all fit fairly comfortably, but they are hats more than a vocation. More than anything else, I enjoy being a pastor at home in my community or being on the road as an itinerant preacher and pastoral troubleshooter.

I have a growing conviction about the need for preaching that would make the gospel known in our historical context, taking a biblical and evangelistic approach with a strong emphasis on conversion. I'm drawn these days to preaching events more than to conferences or workshops; to revivals more than seminars; to sermons more than lectures.

It is time to make preaching the gospel publicly controversial again. We need the kind of preaching that will call people away from the ruling American myths, illusions, and life-style.

A whole new level of public activity for the sake of the poor and for peace could emerge from such preaching, which has a time-tested tradition with deep roots in American history. It is time to reclaim the revival tradition and apply it to the times in which we live, which so desperately cry out for the real preaching of the Word of God.

The possibility of nationwide preaching campaigns has preoccupied my thoughts lately. My hope is that these preaching events will serve a local area, making disciples, building community, creating new energy for the sake of justice and peace.

Above all, it is recovery of faith that is most important. I see Sojourners' call more and more as simply calling people to commitment to Jesus Christ. We began simply with our own relationship to Jesus Christ, grew to see the implications for one another and the church, and can now see hope for a revival that could have far-reaching consequences.

The Call to Conversion

Jim Wallis is convinced that Christian faith is the radical answer to society's search for new life. 'The times in which we live', he writes, 'cry out for our conversion . . . We need nothing less than a spiritual transformation.'

The author is practical and specific in spelling out what this means. The Christian 'good news' speaks of some of the crucial issues which face us today: justice, the bomb, the life of the community. The result is a book which makes fresh, urgent and compelling reading.

'In this superb book, Jim Wallis, one of American Christianity's foremost peace and justice activists and leader in church renewal, dares to make the call to conversion historically specific to the most urgent issues of the 'eighties. It is a clear statement of what it means to be a Christian at the end of the twentieth century.'
Ronald Sider